"*Getting Started with Policy Governance* breathes incredible life into the theory and practice of Policy Governance. This book will open many exciting doors to those who practice its principles or who are sincerely seeking a new way to govern with excellence."

> —**Susan Mogensen,** CEO, International Policy Governance
> Association (IPGA)

"Policy Governance remains the world's most conceptually coherent *theory* of board governance. In her latest book, Caroline Oliver masterfully translates the theory into *practical* application of Policy Governance as a vehicle for boards to help them deal with organisational complexity and bring purpose, integrity, and efficiency to their work. Her ability to communicate potentially complex issues clearly, simply, and succinctly is outstanding."

> —**Stuart Emslie,** CEO, UK Policy Governance Association, and assistant director, London Centre for Corporate Governance and Ethics, Birkbeck, London University

"Caroline Oliver provides proven tools and techniques for maximizing governing performance. With fifteen years of consulting success condensed into one book, it's a must read for anyone working on or with a board."

> —**Ray Tooley,** P.Eng., CEO, OurBoardroom Technologies

"The principles Caroline Oliver outlines in this book were invaluable to us in clarifying the critical distinction between the owner and employee perspectives. I recommend Policy Governance for any employee-owned enterprise wishing to implement a sustainable, ownership-driven governance model."

> —**Mike Haney,** CEO, Athens Group, Inc

"As Mae West once said, 'Too much of a good thing can be wonderful.' Caroline Oliver has provided THE book for boards to use to govern themselves in the best model that exists—the Carver Model. She has cleverly described how boards can make more time for the important things—like why they were formed in the first place and trying to make the world a better place for all of us."

> —**Chris Beth,** 2009–2010 president, California Park and Recreation Society

"Anyone following the events surrounding the financial turmoil in 2007 and 2008 has good reason to wonder if corporate governance is working. Caroline Oliver's latest book provides a route map to an innovative system of governance that boards should find well worth considering and even trying. It also provides many clues as to how some of the recent financial sector problems could have been prevented. Shareholders, too, should be interested in this book, as it is about them, describing a system for how boards steer their organizations in their owners' interests."

> —**Paul Moxey,** head of corporate governance and risk management,
> Association of Certified Chartered Accountants

"This is a great read. Such a book is long overdue: it is comprehensive, accessible, and fills a big gap in the market."

> —**Geraldine Peacock,** CBE, former chair of The Charity Commission of
> England and Wales, UK

Getting Started with Policy Governance

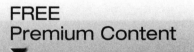

Readers are invited to download and use the Tools from this book provided in electronic format at the Web site address given above.

The Tools are available FREE online as PDF files for printing and, in the case of the forms and checklists offered as Microsoft Word files, for filling out on your computer.

Getting Started with Policy Governance

BRINGING PURPOSE, INTEGRITY, AND EFFICIENCY TO YOUR BOARD

Caroline Oliver

Foreword by
John Carver

JOSSEY-BASS
A Wiley Imprint
www.josseybass.com

Published by Jossey-Bass
A Wiley Imprint
989 Market Street, San Francisco, CA 94103-1741—www.josseybass.com

Jossey-Bass books and products are available through most bookstores. To contact Jossey-Bass directly, call our Customer Care Department within the U.S. at 800-956-7739, outside the U.S. at 317-572-3986, or fax 317-572-4002.

Jossey-Bass also publishes its books in a variety of electronic formats. Some content that appears in print may not be available in electronic books.

Library of Congress Cataloging-in-Publication Data
Oliver, Caroline, date.
    Getting started with policy governance: bringing purpose, integrity, and efficiency to your board/ Caroline Oliver; foreword by John Carver.
        p.   cm.
    Includes bibliographical references and index.
    ISBN 978-0-7879-8713-8 (pbk.)
    1. Boards of directors.   2. Corporate governance.   3. Organizational effectiveness.   I. Title.
    HD2745.O45   2009
    658.4'22—dc22
                                                                                                2008038211

Printed in the United States of America
FIRST EDITION

PB Printing   10 9 8 7 6 5 4 3 2 1

CONTENTS

LIST OF TOOLS

FOREWORD

In *Getting Started with Policy Governance*, Caroline Oliver has once again contributed her keen insights and lucid prose to the growing literature on board leadership. Having coauthored two previous books consistent with the Policy Governance® model on the subject and numerous articles published internationally, here she addresses board members and others linked by interest or livelihood to governance in a way both personal and precise.

Caroline added Policy Governance expertise to her already extensive experience with organizational issues by attending the Policy Governance Academy™ in 1995. The Academy is a five-day intensive experience that Miriam Carver and I conduct and is offered to persons already possessed of considerable Policy Governance knowledge. Of the approximately three hundred governance leaders worldwide who have now gone through this specialized training in the theory and practice of Policy Governance, not one exceeds Caroline in integrity, commitment, and sheer energy devoted to reforming board leadership. She was instrumental in helping to create, then lead, the International Policy Governance Association in 1999 and later the United Kingdom Policy Governance Association in 2006. These membership associations facilitate mutual support, communications, and learning opportunities for Policy Governance consultants and organizations using or considering using the model. Beyond helping organize Policy Governance consultants, Caroline led the charge to have Europe-focused Policy Governance Academies conducted in Britain,

Policy Governance® is the registered service mark of John Carver.

networking feverishly and effectively, as part of her successful efforts to spread Policy Governance in the United Kingdom.

In *Getting Started with Policy Governance,* Caroline takes readers by the hand on a journey through learning about, considering, and implementing the principles of the Policy Governance model. She does so using comparisons and analogies to smooth the conceptual shift from governance-as-usual to governance excellence. She cautions that embarking on an unfamiliar yet compellingly reasonable governance reform will not be easy. She invites us to remember our novice initiation to bicycling with its wobbling, scrapes, and embarrassments as a necessary prelude to expert cycling. As with cycling, governance control that doesn't compromise progress must live in harmony with progress that doesn't compromise control. Wind in our hair without bruises on our knees drives board leadership as well as cycling.

Like all others who teach the Policy Governance model from the Academy's base of understanding, Caroline explains the ends-means distinction, proper policy formulation, balancing board diversity and authoritative unity, chief executive and chief governance positions, and other features of the model. But more than most other writers, Caroline positions her consideration of the board role squarely in the theme of ownership—the legitimacy base of moral authority from which boards govern. She returns to that frequently underappreciated thesis throughout the book, repeatedly drawing the reader's attention back to the whole reason for having boards to begin with. This unrelenting emphasis on an organization's ownership and the board's representative role in owners' interest imparts a unique flavor to this book.

Policy Governance was designed for the fulfillment of governing boards' awesome accountability. A rigorous conceptual framework I developed in the mid-1980s, it departs from the traditional—and still most common—governance approach of simply tacking on an unending sequence of "best practices" without transforming the underlying governance thinking. (All existing corporate governance codes fail to make these underlying changes.) It addresses, on one hand, the nature of the relationship between a large group and its authoritative representative board, council, or commission. On the other hand, it addresses the productive relationship between that representative group and the executive or operational organization. The simple objective is that the representative group—as an active link in the chain of moral authority from owners to operators—causes its organization to perform in a way consistent with an informed summary of owners' wishes.

What sets Policy Governance apart from all other attempts to improve corporate governance is its philosophical and theory-based foundation. Standing alone, as Britain's corporate board pioneer Sir Adrian Cadbury has attested, in its total system approach to board leadership, Policy Governance is a robustly logical answer to the question, "How can a group of equals acting on behalf of others ensure organizational performance accountable to the interests of those owners?" That question is one that has elusively challenged corporate governance, but has been just as thorny a problem for boards of nonprofit organizations and governmental units.

The model is not a structural design but a conceptually coherent set of concepts and principles—sufficient to be called a theory of governance—that apply in any setting where that question arises. No mere Foreword can explain it properly, though other resources are available to do that. My own *Boards That Make a Difference* (Carver, 2006), to which Caroline refers, is one, but her own explanation in these pages also serves the reader well.

At any rate, a corporate board ensures that shareholders' interests are fulfilled by the conduct of business, trade association members' interests are fulfilled by organizational pursuits, and city residents' interests are fulfilled by municipal government action. But as a theory of governance, Policy Governance also carries extensive and largely unexplored implications for political bodies beyond the obvious applications to city councils, boards of education, and other local authorities.

Getting Started with Policy Governance is addressed, of course, to boards of individual organizations. But no one more than Caroline has grasped the utility of Policy Governance principles for the larger world beyond the boardroom. Consequently, Caroline's interest in Policy Governance is of broader scope than its utility considered board by board. Her allegiance to better governance extends to the wide sociopolitical environment that makes organizations and boards possible in the first place. Let me illustrate with a few examples.

As she points out, Policy Governance differentiates between the owners of an organization and the beneficiaries of that organization. Sometimes these roles overlap considerably as, for example, in a trade association. In a democracy with respect to any state, provincial, or national government, citizens are both the owners and most of the beneficiaries. (If a government chooses to grant foreign aid, the foreign countries are beneficiaries though not owners.) It is clear in the Policy Governance paradigm that the governing body is directly linked to owners but not to beneficiaries. The latter are connected not to the board but to the staff or, in the case of governments, the agencies and bureaucracies. Yet citizens, pursuing their own individual interests as government's consumers, will attempt to influence actions the legislature, congress, or parliament should be taking on behalf of the ownership. Without the distinction between these two important but separate roles, elected officials are prone to shortsighted and undemocratic actions. From a Policy Governance perspective, then, legislative bodies would draw a sharp distinction between their duty to citizens as owners and bureaucracies' duty to citizens as beneficiaries.

A closely related implication of Policy Governance concerns lobbyists. As argued by the social contract theory of Jean Jacques Rousseau and embodied in the Policy Governance model, it is the responsibility of the representative body to take the measure of citizens' (as owners) values and desires in an impartial manner, that is, in a way truly representative of the whole. When legislative bodies do not do that (and I argue that none do), they are dependent on specific, highly motivated subsections of the whole for their public input. In no way does the cumulative total of the voices thus heard add up to the whole, nor does it validly represent the whole, the legitimate expression of which Rousseau calls the "general will." Although David Hume, John Stuart Mill, and Rousseau understood the need for smaller groups such as legislatures and councils to legislate on behalf of the public, such groups acting as agents confront the difficulty of knowing the minds of their principals. Groups of citizens—what Rousseau called "partial societies"—band together to have their voices heard; hence the institution of lobbyists. But as Rousseau demonstrates, there is no reason to expect that the general will can be deduced from these partial societies. Worse, lobbies are well known to obstruct elected officials' allegiance to the general will. From a Policy Governance perspective, legislative bodies would minimize or eliminate their dependence on lobbyists, choosing instead to develop and perfect a statistically reliable way to know the minds of those it is their duty to represent.

Moreover, the Policy Governance ends-means distinction has vast implications for governments. Perhaps nowhere else is the confounding of ends and means more damaging to public welfare and the public purse than in national and state or provincial programs. As Caroline explains, Policy Governance causes organizations to be directed by board-stated ends and left free to experiment or choose means limited only by board-stated ethics and prudence boundaries. Yet many, if not most, government pursuits are legislated as means, not as ends, then organized around means more than ends. Consequently, departments of government are massive means machines that derive their funding, their rewards, and their nature from their means rather than from their ends. From a Policy Governance perspective, legislative bodies would broadly prescribe ends and encourage all the creativity that government programs can muster, short of violating clear standards of ethics and prudence.

Similarly, Policy Governance dictates that decision making proceed with a disciplined sequence from broadest expressions of intent toward narrower expressions. As Caroline makes clear, this method also makes delegation easier, since at any point, legislative action can stop and executive action begin. State or provincial legislatures, for example, would never interfere in the way a local school system organizes classes and curricula, though they might well make demands about the levels and types of learning to be produced for the public treasure.

As one final example of the implications of the Policy Governance model beyond the boardroom, there is nothing more crucial than the ethical obligation expressed by terms like *stewardship, agency,* and Robert Greenleaf's *servant-leadership*. There is nothing new about the ideal that elected public servants are just that: public *servants.* Unfortunately that ideal is regularly plundered by elected officials themselves. Yet as long as citizens as beneficiaries make demands for their individual or specific group claims, citizens-as-owners cannot effectively punish political pandering and demand that elected officials not confuse their individual aggrandizement and their individual political brawls with doing the public's business.

The reader can be confident not only that Caroline Oliver conveys clearly the powerful principles that comprise the Policy Governance model, but that she approaches the subject from a wider stance than simply board leadership alone. She writes from a passion for solving the timeless challenge of how we as human beings in large groups can make legitimate, fair, wise decisions for ourselves and our futures.

Atlanta, Georgia   John Carver
October 2008

To my dad,
Michael Dawbarn Oliver,
who showed me the wonder of words and ideas

AUTHOR'S NOTE

Reading Jossey-Bass's "Guidelines for Authors" tells me that this is my "optional" opportunity to frame this book by providing background information and "a more personal picture" of how this book came to be written. I can't resist, not least because I suspect that this may be the last book I write about Policy Governance. This is my third book on the subject, and in it, I attempt to distill everything I have learned in the course of a fascinating journey of almost fifteen years. I am still on that journey, but it is time to move on. I have, at last, done all I need to do to prove to my own satisfaction that Policy Governance, while inevitably not the final word on governance, is a really great place for every board to start. Now I want to devote my time to making it happen on a scale that I and others have so far failed to realize. Other people will, I hope, write more about it; I need to *do* more about it.

Explaining why one man's ideas have gripped me so fiercely is not easy. I often sense that people who know me are disappointed that I am pursuing someone else's ideas and not my own. Yet the thing is, I feel that John Carver's ideas have given me a wonderful impetus for exploring my own ideas without which my own thinking would be nothing like as productive.

Over the last fifteen years, I have read the works of and met and debated with many of the great and good of corporate governance, and never have I found anything that has made me seriously revisit my commitment to furthering Policy Governance. I have come to believe that this is not because I am stupid or blinkered or bigoted but because right now, there is nothing to compare with it. In other words, I honestly believe that if you want a governance *system* today, there is only one, and Policy Governance is it. Maybe other governance systems will emerge, but I am pretty confident that if they do, they will take the form of improvements that emerge from better understanding and use of Policy Governance rather than a completely fresh start.

Therefore, I see no choice for me or my Policy Governance colleagues other than to continue to inform people about this great possibility. Making this choice sometimes feels like being committed to communicating the value of an apple in a world that knows and understands only pears. But it has to be worth it. All the best things in life seem to me to come as a result of the work of small groups—families, teams, boards. If I can continue to help boards—small groups in charge of big ambitions on behalf of all of us—be even a little more effective, I will be fortunate indeed.

October 2008   Caroline Oliver

ACKNOWLEDGMENTS

Although I appear to have written this book alone, it is very much built on experience drawn from working with my earlier coauthors John Carver, Mike Conduff, Susan Edsall, Carol Gabanna, Randee Loucks, Denise Paszkiewicz, Catherine Raso, and Linda Stier. Thank you all for making my writing journey such a fulfilling and enjoyable experience.

The thoughts and work of John and Miriam Carver imbue everything in this book. To say "I couldn't have done it without you" sounds like a cliché, but in this case, it is clearly true. Thank you, John and Miriam, for your generosity and for everything you put into continuing to distinguish the principles and practices that make Policy Governance such a coherent system for organizing governance.

I continue to be inspired by all the people who are giving so much in order to bring Policy Governance to the world. I would like to pay particular tribute to the past and current board members of the International Policy Governance Association—Bill Charney, Mike Conduff, Eric Craymer, Nanci Erkert, Carol Gabanna, Phil Graybeal, Jan Maas, Jannice Moore, Denise Paszkiewicz, Susan Rogers, Linda Stier, and Sue Stratton—and of the U.K. Policy Governance Association—John Bruce, Vijay Mistri, Valerie Moore, Susan Rogers, and Ray Tooley. My deepest thanks also go to the past and present CEOs of both organizations—Howard Stier, Susan Mogensen, and Stuart Emslie—who respectively bring great talent and drive to their work despite a minimum of resources; they are owed a huge debt of gratitude.

My consulting colleagues form a wonderfully supportive community, and many thanks are due to those who have contributed to this book (acknowledged throughout) and to the many more who have offered their help. In particular, Marla Mullen has worked diligently with me to try to explain Executive Limitations as clearly as possible, and my good friend Linda Stier has supported me on every step of the way, her insight and thoughtfulness a constant creative spur.

Estelle Hamoline, far more than my executive coordinator, is a colleague and a friend, and her husband, Raymond Tooley, far more than a business partner, is a constant force for progress and also a friend. I am very grateful to have them both by my side.

Much of the credit for this book must go to my clients, who continue to teach me every day. My consulting experience has involved working with boards of organizations that vary immensely in size, scope, and culture. This book is the direct result of everything I have learned from them. To the extent that this book may help other boards understand what Policy Governance is and how it works, they will have all my previous clients to thank.

I would also like to express my appreciation for the support and encouragement of Dorothy Hearst, Allison Brunner, and Paula Stacey at Jossey-Bass. Paula Stacey deserves a very special mention. She has made numerous highly practical suggestions for improving the original manuscript and given me much direct help in implementing those suggestions. In short, she has been a magnificent and indispensable support, and I shall be forever grateful to her. The road traveled to produce this book has been far from smooth, and our plans have been overtaken time and again by unforeseeable circumstances. Allison Brunner, Jossey-Bass's lead social sector editor, has exercised patience and determination to get through in just the right measures, and I am full of admiration.

Finally, to my family—Ian, Carol, Anna, and Fiona—thank you, with all my heart.

—C.O.

ABOUT THE AUTHOR

CAROLINE OLIVER has been exploring how boards can excel at group leadership for almost fifteen years. Her study of Policy Governance goes back to reading the first edition of John Carver's seminal book *Boards That Make a Difference* in 1994; since then, she has facilitated many hundreds of board interactions, uniting and inspiring boards of all descriptions.

Today, she enjoys bringing all she has learned not only to her consulting work in the United Kingdom, North America, and beyond but also to her writing, which encompasses contributions on governance issues to journals and magazines around the world. She is general editor of *The Policy Governance Fieldbook: Practical Lessons, Tips, and Tools from the Experience of Real-World Boards* (1999) and coauthor, with John Carver, of *Corporate Boards That Create Value: Governing Company Performance from the Boardroom* (2002). Caroline Oliver is founding chair of both the International Policy Governance Association (2000–2005) and the U.K. Policy Governance Association (2006–present). She is chief executive of the international consulting firms Good to Govern and The Governance Corporation and chair of OurBoardroom Technologies Inc., a company dedicated to providing online tools for organizing effective governance process. Further background is available at www.goodtogovern.com, www.thegovernancecorporation.com, and www.ourboardroom.com.

HOW TO USE THIS BOOK

If you are completely new to Policy Governance and want basic information on how it works, I would advise you to start at the beginning and carefully read the first chapter, which gives an overview of Policy Governance. I deliberately wrote this overview in language that will be very familiar to most board members. My aim is to introduce you to the ideas in a way that is as reader-friendly as possible. Next, the chapters on ownership and policy (Chapters Three and Four) will help you understand the fundamental ideas and practices of Policy Governance in more depth.

If your board has some knowledge of Policy Governance and is trying to determine what the next steps are, you will want to explore the process set out in Chapter Two on how to go about deciding whether to adopt Policy Governance. The tools and suggestions that are provided will help your board develop a decision process that it will be comfortable with.

If your board has made the commitment to adopt Policy Governance and wants to get started, this book provides the instruction, tools, and information about additional resources that you need. While I have tried to be comprehensive in taking you through the implementation process—from the steps of crafting policies through how to set up a plan for the first year and monitor your policies—there is no way that a single resource will be enough. For that reason, in the resource section at the end of the book, I include a thorough listing of places to get more information on Policy Governance.

If you are interested in copying and distributing the tools and resources in this book, please feel free. They are available for you to duplicate and use.

You will find the tools referred to in the text at the end of each chapter. You can also find additional resources at www.policygovernanceassociation.org.

Please note that although this book is aimed at potential and actual Policy Governance users across the world, the spellings throughout the book conform to Jossey-Bass's house style, which calls for American English. If you would like any of the tools in other forms of English, please do not hesitate to e-mail me at coliver@goodtogovern.com.

WHY POLICY GOVERNANCE MATTERS

Did you think that governance was boring and dry? Think again. At one level, Policy Governance is no more and no less than a system through which boards can conceptualize, organize, and fulfill their mandate. At another level, it is something that can help fix many of a board's day-to-day problems. But far, far more important, it is a powerful tool through which we all, as global, national, and local citizens, can fulfill our dreams. Through this book, I hope to engage you—whatever type of organization you care about and whether you are a board member, a board officer, or a consultant—in a mind-expanding exploration that will make your leadership as exciting and productive as possible.

Getting Started with Policy Governance

Exploring Policy Governance

Never doubt that a small group of thoughtful, committed citizens can change the world. Indeed, it is the only thing that ever has.

Margaret Mead

Exploring Policy Governance means visualizing an entirely different world of board operation—what it looks like, what it feels like, and what it produces. In this chapter, you are going to learn the basics of what Policy Governance is, how it works, and what you can expect to get from it.

This chapter aims to help you to help your board

- Understand what makes Policy Governance unique as a system for organizing board work
- Understand the basic theory and practice of Policy Governance
- Examine the benefits of Policy Governance

WHAT POLICY GOVERNANCE IS

Policy Governance is a complete system through which boards can conceptualize, organize, and fulfill their mandate. Like all systems, it has several component parts that work together to provide a complete approach to a particular job. A shorthand way of expressing the completeness of the Policy Governance system is to call it a *model*. Thus, in the literature *the Policy Governance model* or *the Carver model,* or sometimes *the Carver Policy Governance model.* Everything in the model fits together because it is an expression of the integrated theory and principles that underlie John Carver's work and that have allowed his approach to become the single most influential model of governance in the world.

Operating from a model that is based on an integrated theory is important in two ways. First, without a fundamental theory guiding your actions, practice will inevitably become haphazard and, ultimately, highly risky for all concerned. Of course, practice is essential, and many of us learn best through concrete experience. But unless practice is derived from theory and the experience derived from practice is used to further inform the theory, how can practice ever be truly practical? In any case, in the same way that it wouldn't be a great idea for a group to tackle a challenge without having some theoretical understanding of the nature of the challenge, it isn't a great idea to start governing without having established some theory about the nature of the board's job that makes sense to everyone. I have seen many boards descend into endless disagreement not because they aren't all wanting to do a good job but because they have no agreed-on theory about what the job is. I have seen many board members who have become apathetic, not because they don't care but because they have tired of trying to make a difference in the midst of confusion. I have seen many boards become totally stuck on board and CEO evaluation issues because they have no agreement about what good performance looks like.

The second reason for operating from a model that is based on a theory that integrates all board work has to do with efficiency. By definition, the value of working from a complete model rather than from a collection of best practices is that all the parts of a model are specifically designed to work together. For example, when you are flying in an airplane, driving a car, or riding a bike, you know that you need all its components to be working together in order to get you safely to where you want to go. Similarly, when you are governing an organization, you need to be sure that as far as possible, everything you are doing is working together to get your organization going safely to where you want it to go. Boards are complex mechanisms involving the energies of chairs, board members, CEOs, staff, and external stakeholders. With a complete model, everyone's role, purpose, and practices can be aligned toward the same ends. Without a complete model, people usually find themselves and their practices pulling in different directions.

Everything about the Policy Governance system aims to help boards enable their organization to achieve their goals as efficiently and effectively as possible. This book aims to help you understand and use that system to best effect. One device that I will use in this book is the creation of analogies, for I believe that in likening the unfamiliar to the familiar, analogies can often be helpful in developing understanding of something new. It's helpful to think of Policy Governance as a vehicle that your board can use to get where it wants to go. In particular, let's observe some important points by examining how using Policy Governance is like riding a bicycle:

- Like a bicycle, Policy Governance is a vehicle, a means of getting wherever you choose to go. It is not a destination.

- Walking and riding a bike are two entirely different modes of travel. Similarly, governing with traditional tools and governing with Policy Governance are two entirely different modes of operation.

- Riding a bike, like using Policy Governance, does not feel natural before it is learned, but once fully experienced, it is never forgotten.

- Learning to ride a bike, like learning to operate through Policy Governance, requires having the courage to *entirely* let go of one form of control in order to gain a different form of control.

- Once you have learned to ride a bike, you can ride any bike to any destination. Similarly, once you have learned Policy Governance, you can use it on any governing body.

As with any new skill, mastery of bicycle riding—and of Policy Governance— is a function of practice.

ACCOUNTABILITY TO OWNERSHIP: THE THEORY THAT DRIVES POLICY GOVERNANCE

In the same way that the benefits of cycling are the result of all a bike's component parts working together, the benefits that Policy Governance offers are the result of the careful creation of a complete system. Policy Governance starts with a theory. This theory drives certain understandings about the board's job, which eventually translate into movement toward the organization's goals.

Ownership: The Power Behind Your Wheels

The theory or belief that lies behind Policy Governance is that organizations exist to fulfill their owners' purposes and that boards exist to represent those owners. Therefore, Policy Governance theory asserts that the power that propels any board forward should be its interpretation of the best interests of the owners of its organization.

Given that board power is owners' power, it follows that clarity about who an organization's owners are is fundamental. For corporations and their shareholders, as well as for membership associations and their members, the meaning of *ownership* seems obvious. For many nonprofit and public organizations, however, it is often not at all clear and, therefore, needs to be defined by the board.

Policy Governance theory positions ownership as both a legal and a moral issue. Legally, your organization's owners are the people who, according to your bylaws, have the right to vote at general or special meetings of shareholders or members. However, your board can also choose to define a much wider moral ownership that includes everyone to whom it feels it should be accountable, which might include many others whom your board sees as actually or potentially invested in your organization's long-term future in some shape or form. For example, the board of a food bank might well have a legal ownership that consists of board members alone but decide to operate as if it were accountable to either its entire local community or a subset of the community such as "all those who care about poverty."

A board can only begin to truly govern if it can identify its owners—the people on whose behalf it is governing. And they must not confuse owners with other stakeholders such as customers and employees. A board that sees itself as governing on behalf of its owners will collectively shoulder responsibility for the proper care of its organization in the interests of *all* current and future beneficiaries. A board whose members see themselves as individual representatives of particular interests will not.

The significance of ownership will be explored in far more detail in Chapter Three but is summarized in the following list:

Owners are . . .

- the source of the board's authority
- the people to whom the board is accountable

- a touchstone for and ultimate legitimizers of board decisions and actions
- a force for unifying the board in common cause
- the most likely source of future board leadership
- essential for stability and sustainability
- a protection against warring self-interests
- concerned about the care of the overall organization

Accountability: The Chain That Brings Power to Your Wheels

Having identified owners' best interests as the power that you should be using to drive your wheels, you need to connect that power to the wheels that can move your board and your organization forward. Policy Governance is designed to provide that connection through a chain of accountability, as follows:

1. The board as a group must connect with and be accountable to the source of its authority: its owners.

2. The board must interpret its owners' best interests in order to define what the organization is for and how it should operate.

3. The board must ensure that the organization performs according to its interpretation of its owners' best interests.

VALUES INTO ACTION: THE WORKING PARTS OF POLICY GOVERNANCE

Having created the chain of accountability that connects the power of your owners' best interests through your board to your organization, you have to actually turn the wheels and go. In other words, you have to put the theory into practice. This brings us to what we might call the "moving parts" of Policy Governance—the components that make the organization move. These components, essentially, are actions that the board needs to take.

Define the Difference Your Owners Want to Make

The Policy Governance system starts from where owners start—that is, from an overall perspective in which the organization is merely a vehicle for delivering the benefit that they seek. As the owners' representative, your board's main purpose is to ensure that what owners want their organization to produce gets produced. In other words, what matters to boards about the organizations that they govern are the external impacts they make, not the means of making them. This does not translate into saying that boards have no interest in means at all. It does translate into saying that if boards fail to keep everyone's focus on the reason for everything they do, the doing will quickly go awry.

To put the Policy Governance system into practice, boards have to identify the difference their owners want their organization to make, not in terms of what the organization is going to do but in terms of the impact it is going to have on people's lives. This involves answering three questions:

1. What benefits should your organization produce?

2. For whom?

3. With what cost-efficiency?

In the Policy Governance system, the answers to these questions form your organization's *Ends.* Whether you call them *Ends* or something else really doesn't matter as long as you have answered all three questions at some level.

You will find a lot more on Ends in Chapter Five. For now, the important things to understand are that Ends are essentially what you want your organization to achieve and that whereas most boards typically address this issue by creating a mission statement and approving a strategic plan, in Policy Governance, boards are asked to be more rigorous. Answering the three Ends questions is not easy, but unless they are clearly answered by the board, the organization will, to some degree, be rudderless and its accountability therefore hazy.

Assign Responsibility for Making That Difference

The next step in the Policy Governance system is for the board to determine who it is going to make responsible for achieving its Ends. In doing so, it is obliged to recognize that it remains ultimately accountable to its owners for everything, including Ends accomplishment, whether or not it delegates responsibility to others to get the work done. Most boards choose to operate through a chief executive officer (CEO) as the sole connector between the board and management, and the remainder of this book assumes that choice. Other possible choices are discussed on pages 139–140 in Chapter Seven, and the board chair's role is discussed briefly later in this chapter and at greater length in subsequent chapters. Having an intact chain of accountability in which everyone is clear about who has overall day-to-day responsibility for getting the Ends accomplished (whether or not that person—or those persons—further delegate elements of the job) is an essential component of the Policy Governance system. Having a CEO is not.

Limit the Authority That Goes with the Responsibility as Minimally as You Can

To accomplish your Ends with the greatest possible velocity, your CEO needs to be free to take the quickest route available at any time, unless doing so would put the organization in ethical or legal jeopardy. In the Policy Governance system, the board's ethical and prudential limits are typically called *Executive Limitations* but can be called whatever your board decides as long as they always address things that cannot be allowed rather than how things should be done. Chapter Six gives more detailed information about creating Executive Limitations.

Put Everything in Comprehensive Yet Concise Written Policy

Your board members might currently think of policies as rules, standards, guidelines, or principles. They might also think of policies as procedures that set out the way you do things or as a framework for the way you do your work. If you are a political party or government, you might also think of policy as the high-level plan or course of action that lies behind your legislative decisions on a particular issue. There is no one definition. *Policy* is a word that is used in many different ways. Policies in the Policy Governance system are values specifically designed to enable your board to be accountable for everything about your organization. The design has three elements.

First, the policies need to be *written* because owners' authority has been given to your board as a group and, therefore, unless you will be meeting in permanent session, you need a form of control that works whether or not you are all in the building. Concretizing or codifying your control in agreed-on written policies—a permanently accessible set of instructions—is the answer.

Second, board policy must also be *comprehensive* if it is to cover everything that the board is accountable for, which is, indeed, everything! In the Policy Governance system, the board's policies are divided into four categories that, between them, cover all possible board concerns. The first category is typically called Ends, as described earlier. The second category is typically called Executive Limitations, as described earlier. Together these represent the entirety of your board's instructions to your CEO. The remaining policies are your board's instructions to itself. As such, they could be combined in one category. However, for the sake of clarity, they are typically divided between a category called *Governance Process* and another called *Board-Management Delegation.* You can find more about alternative names for the four policy categories on pages 77–79 in Chapter Four.

Third, an essential component of the Policy Governance system is that policy in each of the four categories is *created from the broadest to the narrowest level of specificity.* Here's why: if you think about the number of policies any given board could have in the four categories, your head is likely to start spinning. John Carver, the originator of Policy Governance, once memorably remarked that "brevity is the unsung hallmark of leadership." And you can see his reason. After a certain point, too much policy means less control, not more. Unless you have the time and expertise to manage the number and complexity of the policies you create and unless you can reasonably afford the cost of monitoring them, you may certainly have policies but you certainly will not have *policy control.*

The Policy Governance system makes brevity possible by requiring you to create policies in each of the four categories from the top—in other words, from the broadest ownership viewpoint rather than from the viewpoint of someone working within the organization. By *broadest,* I mean that your policy in each category must start with a statement that encompasses everything you want to say in that category, so that no part of your accountability is left out. The first policy you create in each category therefore covers every possible further topic within that category at the most inclusive level.

For example, in the Executive Limitations category, when you address your CEO's means, you will probably want first to create a broad statement that ensures that your CEO will not compromise your organization's legal, financial, or ethical health.

Thereafter, your board will create further policies, progressively narrowing the range of options for interpreting policy until you are satisfied that you can safely leave further interpretation up to your CEO. You will find further explanation of the concept of defining policies from the broadest to the narrowest in Chapter Four.

Delegate Within "Any Reasonable Interpretation"

At the point when your board members decide that their policies say all that is needed in order to fulfill their obligation to owners, those to whom the board has delegated the responsibility for fulfilling the policies can get going and keep going as long as they are operating within those policies. "Operating within those policies" means something very specific for delegates in the Policy Governance system. It means that they must always be in a position to prove that they are operating within any reasonable interpretation of their board's policies.

As noted earlier, your board's delegate with respect to fulfillment of your Ends and Executive Limitations policies is typically your organization's CEO, whom you may call your *chief executive, managing director,* or any other title. With respect to fulfillment of your Governance Process and Board-Management Delegation policies, your delegate is likely to be called your *chair, president,* or, as suggested by the Carvers, *chief governance officer* (CGO), which is the title that will primarily be used in this book.

Thus, the Policy Governance system enables a very clear distinction between the CEO and CGO roles. Each person has their own domain of interpretation. Your CEO has the right to make any reasonable interpretation of your Ends and Executive Limitations, and your CGO has the right to make any reasonable interpretation of your Governance Process and Board-Management Delegation policies. Both lead in their own domain, and both are free to play their role to the full as long as they are operating within any reasonable interpretation of what your board requires of them.

Be Sure You Are Making the Difference Your Owners Want

Policy control is only real if your policies are used, and you can't know that they are being used unless you monitor them. To use the Policy Governance system, your board will need to establish schedules for regular monitoring of each of its policies and for regular CEO and board evaluations based on that monitoring. Monitoring policies will be discussed in depth in Chapter Seven.

So there you have it—a brief overview of the Policy Governance system. If you would like more information, refer to the list of Policy Governance resources at the back of this book. For now, let's look at the benefits of using Policy Governance.

THE BENEFITS OF USING POLICY GOVERNANCE

So what could your board get from using Policy Governance? Going back to the bike analogy, none of us would have bothered to learn to ride unless we saw the benefits of doing so. But we did see those benefits. We saw our friends using their newfound freedom to move with velocity to wherever they chose.

We saw the pleasure and satisfaction they were getting along the way, and although we had no idea what the feeling of being able to ride was, we knew we wanted to master it, too.

Although it is true that some boards become interested in exploring Policy Governance because they find themselves in some sort of difficulty, many boards explore Policy Governance simply out of an interest in seeing whether it can be a means of improving their performance. In other words, exploring Policy Governance is not necessarily about *needing* something; it is about seeing whether something more is possible.

Especially since the publication of John Carver's *Boards That Make a Difference* in 1990, boards of all sorts have been working with Policy Governance. The benefits they have gained have yet to be academically researched (see page 28 in Chapter Two), but they have been studied through reviewing the experience of eleven organizations in *The Policy Governance Fieldbook* (Oliver and others, 1999) and experienced firsthand by a growing body of board members, executives, and professional consultants, including, over the last fifteen years, me. The following picture of the benefits that boards can obtain from using Policy Governance has emerged.

Become a Real Leadership Team

Imagine your board as a real leadership team. Using Policy Governance would require your board to establish a set of common beliefs about who you all work for and what you should be doing on their behalf. Through that process, you can become a forward-thinking, proactive team that focuses your organization on its long-term purpose and results. It no longer matters how each of you got onto the board because now that you are there, you all have the same job to do for the same people. Your diversity, instead of pulling you apart, becomes a valuable asset for better decision making on behalf of all the people you collectively represent.

Get Where You Want to Go

If you don't know where you want to get to, you definitely won't get there. Using Policy Governance, your board will become crystal clear about where it wants your organization to get to. You won't be managing day-to-day matters. You will be deciding how people's lives should be changed as a result of your organization's existence. Maybe children will be safe from harm. Maybe people will breathe clean air. Maybe financial investors will get a particular return on their investment. Maybe members of your trade association will have the conditions needed for their success.

Get There Faster

Policy Governance offers a quantum leap in board effectiveness, a leap made possible by a governing system that ensures that an organization has a crystal clear direction *and* the freedom it needs to move in that direction with maximum velocity while complying with appropriate standards of ethics and prudence. Thus, you can visualize the experience of sitting on a Policy Governance board as being much like the experience of riding a bike. Once you have mastered Policy Governance, you know that you can steer your organization where you want with a minimal shift of the steering wheel, and the only thing that need slow you down is the occasional application of your brakes for safety. In other words, Policy Governance offers the possibility of fulfilling your ends as soon as possible within reasonable bounds of safety.

Have the Control *and* the Freedom You Need

Your board needs to be in control—to pin things down, to measure, question, and assess them. But your board also needs to give itself the space to explore and create the future and give your CEO and staff the freedom to use their talents and skills to fulfill that future. Policy Governance offers the possibility of achieving an optimal balance between freedom and control—between vision and compliance, between understeering and oversteering.

Your control will be leveraged through grounding everything about your organization in a firm, clear, consistent, comprehensive but brief policy framework that guides everyone through good times and bad. The space for your board and your staff to create and fulfill the future will be made available through efficient board process and clear, safe delegation.

Be Clear About Who Does What

In a hospital operating room, being clear about who does what may make the difference between life and death. The consequences of role confusion in your organization may not be as obvious or dramatic as they are in an operating room, but there are consequences, and they aren't good. Using Policy Governance will give your board the ability to separate governance and management issues so that your board and your CEO can move forward powerfully—individually and together.

Know How Well You Are All Doing

Does your board know whether your organization is making more of a difference today than it was making a couple of years ago? You may know whether
the organization is busier, and you may know whether you have more staff, but
until and unless you know whether you are making more of the kind of difference that you want to make, you cannot jump to any conclusions. Using Policy
Governance will give your board clear and common benchmarks for success and
safety that can be used to evaluate board and CEO performance.

Be Seen to Be Great

Your board is no doubt acutely aware of the ever-increasing expectations of governance regulators and commentators along the lines of "boards must do better." Maybe your board has also noticed the lack of practical suggestions about
how boards are supposed to meet these increased expectations. Currently, Policy
Governance seems to be unique in setting out a comprehensive set of practical
steps that every board can take to fulfill its mandate. This book will set forth
those steps in detail in subsequent chapters.

With Policy Governance installed, your board will be able to readily demonstrate governing excellence to regulators and stakeholders alike; transparency,
foresight, and accountability will be the hallmarks of your leadership.

MOVING ON

Policy Governance is not complicated or hard, but it isn't automatic, either. In
the same way that riding a bike seems entirely unnatural until you know how to
do it, using a governing system that requires letting go of your previous ways of
doing things can seem a bit alarming. But however many hours you may spend
on a tricycle or with training wheels or with your dad holding onto your bike
seat, one day you will have to let go of those things entirely if you are going to
become the rider of your bike. Similarly, learning about Policy Governance is a
long way from actually using Policy Governance; the problem is that in order to
make it work, you will have to stop doing what you have been doing and actually use it. The next chapter is about helping your board to decide whether it
wishes to use Policy Governance, which involves looking more closely at the gap
between traditional board practice and Policy Governance and at what might
enable your board to decide to take that leap.

Choosing Policy Governance—or Not!

> *Only human beings guide their behaviour by a knowledge of*
> *what happened before they were born and a preconception of what may*
> *happen after they are dead; thus only humans find their way by a light*
> *that illuminates more than the patch of ground they stand on.*

Peter Medawar and Jean Medawar, *The Life Science*

The last chapter was designed to help you conduct your initial exploration of what the Policy Governance system is. This chapter provides advice and resources to help your board with the process of deciding whether you want to use Policy Governance.

Reading this chapter will enable you to help your board

- Decide how to decide
- Review different approaches to board leadership
- Plan further learning about Policy Governance
- Identify its governance goals
- Assess the likely rewards and costs of change

- Consider the importance of your history
- Address typical concerns about change
- Decide whether to invest in creating your first set of policies under Policy Governance

DECIDING HOW TO DECIDE!

The first thing is to decide what process you are going to use to make the decision. Many decisions get bogged down because people are unhappy with the process. Disagreements usually crop up because people have different data, different assumptions, or different goals; in other words, they are coming from different contexts. So laying the groundwork for a good decision involves setting the context, which means being very clear about the data you are going to obtain and share, as well as the assumptions and goals that you are all bringing to the table. A typical decision-making process is outlined in Tool 2.1 at the end of this chapter. Your board might want to tailor this process for its own purposes.

REVIEWING YOUR CURRENT APPROACH
TO BOARD LEADERSHIP

In exploring whether Policy Governance is for them, the members of your board are likely to want to know more not only about Policy Governance but also about what the alternatives are. Determining the alternatives involves looking at your current approach to governance as well as what other approaches are being used by other boards.

Of course, the approach your board members will be most familiar with is the one they are using today, and it will probably be useful for you to analyze that approach so that you become conscious of its benefits and shortfalls. You may find that in fact your board members have very different starting assumptions about governance. To uncover your board's current assumptions about governance, you might want to consider using a tool such as the questionnaire at the end of this chapter (Tool 2.2). It is probably a good idea to let each person complete the questionnaire individually and then let everyone know how many people chose each response to each question. Anonymous processes are extremely helpful in laying the groundwork for board discussions, for they enable people to speak with and hear each other freely.

Understanding your organization's history can also help your board recognize how you arrived at the governance approach you are using today. In the early days of almost any organization, there is a stage in which the distinctions between ownership, board, and management are all but nonexistent because the founder plays all of those roles. There is also a stage at which many boards, particularly in nonprofit organizations, use committees (partly or wholly) as management rather than as governance helpers. With these kinds of histories, it is hardly surprising that boards find it hard to contemplate a system that is designed to enable a clear delineation of owner, governor, and executive roles. Yet even for a solely owned enterprise at the earliest stage, Policy Governance can be used to distinguish each role and play each out to beneficial effect. For example, owners of small stores who see themselves only in an executive role are likely to permanently restrict themselves to having a very small business. Similarly, groups of volunteers who band together to do great things in their community but fail to distinguish their need to govern from their need to do are unlikely to grow into mature organizations. In other words, board members who can see that their organizations require the roles of governor and owner to be played to the full are much more likely to do what it takes to separate their roles as employees and thereby create the capacity to expand.

It can also be useful to consider the history of board operation itself. Where did the "rules" the board uses today come from? The answer is usually that they have come from all over the place. Boards of today did not create the rules they are living by today; they inherited them, and ultimately, subject only to the voice of society as expressed by the legislators and regulators of our respective lands and the voice of their owners as expressed in their bylaws, boards have every right—indeed, we could say the responsibility—to make the rules that they believe will best serve their governing purpose.

As you review your current approach to board leadership, it might be helpful to have in mind the different ideas that can underlie board members' current assumptions. Looking carefully at how governance is approached today by your board members and others, you are likely to see several different but often overlapping ideas about the board's job.

Watchdog

Agency theory addresses the gap between principals and their agents in terms of actual and potential conflicts of interest (Alchian and Demsetz, 1972; Jensen and Meckling, 1976; Eisenhardt, 1989). From this perspective, boards operate in the gap between owners and operators, and their job is to act as a watchdog, inspecting and approving in order to prevent any malfeasance. The dominance of this approach has no doubt increased, particularly in widely held corporations, aided by corporate scandals at Enron and elsewhere, as evidenced by the Sarbanes-Oxley Act in the United States and the attendant rush of new regulations and codes around the world.

Advisor

Stewardship theory is less well defined but tends to see the gap between principals and their agents, at least in part, as involving actual or potential CEO incompetence. From this perspective, the board's job is to be the CEO's coach, reviewing, advising, and guiding as well as opening doors to new markets and providing needed expertise in particular areas (for example, legal issues, marketing, international development, information technology, or accounting). This approach is very common in closely held corporations such as those with a controlling shareholder, family firms, and joint ventures.

Assistant

A third paradigm is that the CEO provides the real overall leadership. From this perspective, the board is the CEO's supporter, helping out with networking and resource development. This type of board is typically found early in an organization's life cycle or in small privately held corporations.

Constituent's Advocate

Some board members, particularly many of those operating in the public sector, see their job as battling for the competing interests of the constituencies from which they were elected. In such instances, it can seem to an outside observer that the success of the board as a group authority is a matter of indifference to its members and that personal success in the form of re-election is their main agenda.

Governor

While the term *governor* can mean different things to different people (encompassing some or all of the ideas just reviewed), I am using it to describe the paradigm that Policy Governance comes from. In this paradigm, the board's job is viewed as the expression of ownership within an organization. From this perspective, the board's job is to ensure that owners get what they want with as much velocity as can be achieved within the level of risk that they can tolerate.

LEARNING ABOUT POLICY GOVERNANCE
AND OTHER APPROACHES

As I mentioned in Chapter One, the Policy Governance system is often called a *model*, indicating that like all systems, it comprises several component parts that work together to provide a *complete* approach to a particular job. Reviewing alternatives to Policy Governance carries with it the problem of agreeing on what is and is not a real alternate model as opposed to just a different approach.

In order to give you the maximum possible range of exploration, the following terms have been associated with particular governance approaches that your board may wish to contrast and compare with Policy Governance:

Administrative	Knowledge based
Adolescent	Last resort
Advisory	Life cycle
Balanced scorecard for boards	Management
Collective	Market
Committee	Mature
Community	Membership
Community driven	Mission based
Complementary	Operational
Constituency representative	Participatory
Contingency	Partnership
Corporate	Patron
Cultural trustees handbook	Peter Drucker
Cupped hands	Philanthropic
Dynamic	Policy
Effective	Political
Emergent cellular	Relationship
Established	Representational
Executive	Results based
Founding	School board effectiveness
Fundraising	Stakeholder
Governance as leadership	Traditional
High impact	Venture
Hybrid	Volunteer
Infant	Working
Institutional	Zoning commission
Junior	

Of course, your board may be clear that Policy Governance is the only approach that it wants to spend time considering. In either case, some of the background research can be delegated to board committees or the work can be divided between all board members.

A note of caution for those who embark on a search for alternative governance models: clearly, it would be great if boards had a variety of governance models to choose from, and I hope that one day they will, but I am afraid that the truth is that any research you do today is unlikely to produce anything that really compares with the Policy Governance model as a total operating system. This fact means that the question your board is most likely to face is not "Which of these models should we choose?" but rather "Do we want to use the Policy Governance model or a variety of insights and recommendations from other approaches and sources?"

For information about Policy Governance, all the chapters in this book as well as the list of Policy Governance resources at the end of this book should provide you with plenty of material that you may wish to share with your board. Given the fact that there is so much material, you may want to start by agreeing on the information you will obtain for a preliminary discussion before potentially proceeding to a second stage for which you would obtain more data. It is useful to remember that learning as a board by definition needs to engage people with a range of learning styles. All of us represent some combination of different styles, so learning is most likely to be successful for your board if the information is provided in formats that suit a variety of learning styles. For example, some people learn best through individual study of books and articles, while others may get more out of group presentations or interviews with people who are using Policy Governance. If you are interested in exploring the various learning styles of board members and the kinds of formats that might be a good fit, there is more information in Tool 2.3 at the end of this chapter.

Whatever information you choose to gather about Policy Governance or other approaches, your board is going to need some criteria for choosing its way forward. In other words, you need to know what your board wants to achieve with *any* approach it uses. You need to know your *governance goals*. In Tool 2.4 at the end of this chapter, you will find an approach to goal setting that starts by having the board consider its current performance in a few key areas. From there, it should be a relatively simple job for board members to analyze what they have learned about what different governance approaches offer in relation to their goals. In particular, if you want to compare Policy Governance with other approaches, you might want to ask these questions:

- What does this approach aim to achieve, and how do these aims fit with our governance goals?
- What evidence is there that this approach achieves its aims?
- What education and training resources exist for boards interested in pursuing this approach?
- Who can we talk to who has experience in using this approach?

ASSESSING THE REWARDS AND COSTS OF CHANGING TO POLICY GOVERNANCE

Change of any sort is likely to bring rewards and costs, and your board will want to consider those. A change to Policy Governance is far greater than a change to most, if not all of the current alternatives, for Policy Governance is an entirely new system of governance designed to produce comprehensive accountability to owners rather than to fit with traditional board practice. Therefore, if your board is attracted by the benefits set forth in Chapter One, it may well need to be prepared to make significant changes. Table 2.1 summarizes the kinds of changes that may be required. You may not be starting from the extreme represented by the left-hand side, but wherever you are starting from, if you choose to use Policy Governance, the right-hand column is where you should arrive.

It is inevitable that there will be some costs of change that you will need to weigh against the benefits. In choosing whether to incur such costs, the board is doing a job that no one else can do for it. And whatever choice is made, the responsibility for its consequences are the board's and the board's alone. Given that responsibility, it is essential that members of your board look carefully before leaping, using its goals for governance as suggested in the preceding section. For example, if one of your goals is to give your CEO clearer direction, you need to consider if that would make changing to Policy Governance worthwhile. And remember, you can choose to make the choice by considering what seems right for you as individual board members of today or by considering what you all think is right for your owners in the long run. Some will tell you that to think only of the former is to shortchange your owners; others will tell you that to think of the latter without taking full account of the former is a route fraught with danger. You have to decide.

Table 2.1
From Traditional Board Practice to Policy Governance

TRADITIONAL PRACTICE	POLICY GOVERNANCE
Compliance-driven	Vision-driven
Inwardly focused	Outwardly focused
Short-term view	Long-term view
Mainly considers reports	Mainly considers the future
Command and control	Empowerment and safety
Approval without stated criteria	Pre-stated criteria
Lots of approvals	Pre-approved if criteria are met
Judgment without stated criteria	Judgment against pre-stated criteria
More rules	Fewer rules
Pinning things down	Freeing things up

Trading traditional practice for Policy Governance means

LETTING GO OF . . .	AND GETTING . . .
Giving advice to a delegate unless it is clear that they can reject it without any implications for subsequent performance evaluation	The ability to relate freely to delegates because you are secure in the policy framework that governs your respective roles
Making decisions without reviewing what you have already said in policy	Ever more thoughtful policies
	Effective use of time on new rather than old issues
"Approving" budgets and strategic plans	Budgets and strategic plans that are designed to produce what the board wants produced
Control exercised on the basis of "understandings" between individuals	Control exercised on the basis of explicit policy created by the whole board
The need for many things to be referred to the board for a decision	Greatest possible delegation
Meetings on issues of the moment, with regular reporting on matters of executive concern	Regular reporting on all board concerns
Not meaning what you say	A solid social contract

Time and Money

Costs of time and money will need to be invested in learning about Policy Governance and in developing your policies. And once you have created your policies, you have to keep investing in them—using them, monitoring them, reviewing them, and refreshing your understanding of their structure and purpose—or you will inevitably lose them. Tool 2.5 at the end of this chapter is designed to help you assess the likely potential costs of time and money that will be required. Some of the terms in this tool may be unfamiliar to you at this stage, but they will be more fully explained in later chapters. Bear in mind that all of the time estimates are approximate and may well need to be revised upward (unlikely downward) depending on the amount of discussion your board requires.

Board Turnover

When a board institutes Policy Governance, there may be some cost in terms of board members who leave or become disaffected because they are not comfortable with the board's new mode of operation. Generally, board members who are comfortable using the Policy Governance system tend to have certain perspectives and competencies. The following list, based on one provided by John Carver (personal communication, 2008), may help you assess the likely cost in terms of impact on current board members.

Board members who can adapt well to Policy Governance

- Understand board members' trustee role on behalf of ownership as a whole
- Are committed to the organization's area of concern
- Tend to think in terms of systems and context
- Are able to deal with values, vision, and the long term
- Enjoy dealing with values, vision, and the long term
- Are able and willing to participate assertively in deliberation and abide by the intent of established policies
- Are willing to share power in group process
- Are willing to delegate substantial amounts of decision making to others

Focus and Discipline

Instituting Policy Governance involves some cost related to the sheer focus and effort it takes to govern in such a deliberate and conscious manner. Under Policy Governance, it is much harder to get away with just turning up at the board meeting having read your papers on the way in. Policy Governance doesn't make governance a tough job, but it does confront us with its full meaning and responsibilities and requires a level of self-discipline on the board that goes far beyond the norm.

The Cost of Staying Put

What would be the cost to your board of staying as you are? You don't want to forget the concerns that you may have about how your board is operating today. While there are costs in making the change to a new system that requires a commitment of time, resources, focus, and discipline, there is also a cost in continuing as you are. A questionnaire at the end of this chapter poses some questions that will help your board assess the cost of not making the change to Policy Governance (see Tool 2.6).

IDENTIFYING AND ADDRESSING BOARD MEMBERS' QUESTIONS AND CONCERNS

A vital part of your discussion will involve addressing board members' questions and concerns. Unless all questions and concerns are fully and frankly discussed, the board will have failed to do its job. In any case, if you are trying to facilitate your board's process, it is important to focus both on getting everyone involved and on handling every question respectfully; you'll never know how many others in the room have exactly the same issue. In other words, your job is to focus on hearing from and communicating with the people who aren't speaking. Everyone else is already doing their job!

Here are some ideas for setting about the task of getting all the questions and concerns on the table.

Getting Concerns on the Table

Many of us operate much of the time from the maxim (attributed variously to Groucho Marx, George Eliot, Albert Einstein, and others), "It is better to remain silent and be thought a fool than to open your mouth and remove all doubt."

From the owners' viewpoint, however, a board member who has something to say but does not say it is failing them. Owners have given their authority to *all* board members in order to achieve a level of diversity—and therefore a richness of dialogue—that they hope will do them all justice. Again, in this process of voicing concerns, anonymous processes that engage the full board can be immensely helpful. Tool 2.7, at the end of this chapter, outlines a process for ensuring that all members have a chance to air their concerns.

Table 2.2 provides a summary of typical concerns that board members have about Policy Governance, as well as information on how to address these concerns. Many of these concerns are also addressed more fully in the next section, which explores frequently asked questions.

Susan Mogensen, CEO of the International Policy Governance Association, which brings together a wide array of Policy Governance practitioners, has come up with a novel idea for handling board members' questions about Policy Governance: If you can get hold of someone who has particularly good knowledge of Policy Governance (it will need be very good knowledge!), why not put them on trial? "The Trial of Miss Polly C. Governance" can be as simple as inviting board members to prepare questions and take turns asking Miss Polly C. to answer them, or it can be set up as a more elaborate exercise with prosecution and defense teams as well as a jury.

Frequently Asked Questions

Board members will have lots of questions, some arising from what they have heard about Policy Governance in the past. In any case, concerns are inevitable when board members are considering a system to help them do something that they have previously "just done" without thinking about it. It is vital to avoid assuming the worst of those who do have concerns. That person who might appear lazy may have a legitimate concern that his or her colleagues are not willing or able to devote the needed time and effort to installing Policy Governance. That other person who might appear to be micromanaging for the sake of personal control may have a legitimate concern about specific items that the board should not fail to see or address. The following answers to board members' frequently asked questions may help; in addition, see Tool 8.4 at the end of Chapter Eight, which addresses risk. And don't forget that the index of this book will point you toward answers for most other questions and concerns that may arise in your discussions.

Table 2.2
Typical Concerns About Policy Governance

CONCERN	DIAGNOSIS	POSSIBLE ACTIONS
"Individual board members should be able to say or do anything they want and therefore cannot be subject to any system."	This is a common concern of board members who see their duty as being a one-person watchdog or as representing individual constituents or subsets of the whole ownership.	1. Consider the cost of handling board member and constituent concerns in an ad hoc manner as opposed to handling them through a system devised on behalf of the whole ownership (see p. 61 in Chapter Three and p. 184 in Chapter Eight). 2. Understand the treatment of individual board member and constituent issues in Policy Governance (see p. 184 in Chapter Eight).
"It's unfamiliar, which makes me feel anxious—not a good feeling for a board member!"	This person may be quite keen to move to Policy Governance but is asking you to help them find a level of comfort.	1. Adapt some of the language (see pp. 77–79 in Chapter Four). 2. Highlight other boards like yours that are using Policy Governance. 3. Provide more information about what practicing Policy Governance looks and feels like from an individual board member's perspective (see pp. 180–181 in Chapter Eight).
"I am not sure I am the right person for this new job."	This person is not necessarily against the move but needs more information to understand what their new role will look like.	1. Give more information about what practicing Policy Governance looks and feels like from an individual board member's perspective (see pp. 180–181 in Chapter Eight). 2. Look at alternate ways in which this board member's existing contributions can usefully continue (see p. 170 in Chapter Eight).
"Aren't systems by definition inhuman?"	This person is concerned that formalizing roles will interfere with free and open collegiality.	1. Give more information about the freedom that Policy Governance gives to board, CEO, and board-CEO-staff relationships. 2. Have this board member interview other organizations that use Policy Governance.

Who Else Is Using Policy Governance?   Boards of all types and sizes in North America, Europe, and beyond are using Policy Governance. No directory currently exists, but a Web search on the words *Policy Governance* or *Carver governance* and inquiries through the International Policy Governance Association (IPGA) or board consultants in your area may help you find boards similar to your own. You can find information on the IPGA in the Policy Governance Resources section at the end of the book.

Can Policy Governance Work for All Boards?   This question can be asked as a matter of theory or practice. The design of the Policy Governance system is universal because it provides a container—not the content—for the effective organization of any board's values. Every board that uses Policy Governance remains unique. It's just that all of those boards are using a common system to organize the governance of their organizations, in the same way that we all use the same annual calendaring system to organize our unique personal lives. Therefore, in theory, Policy Governance can work for all boards.

To answer the question of whether Policy Governance can work for all boards in practice, we can go back to our bike analogy. If no one pedals your bike or if parts are missing or fitted in a way that is inconsistent with the purpose of the design, your bike will not work properly. Similarly, if for any reason your board doesn't do what it takes to use Policy Governance properly, the system can't work. Otherwise, as shown by the wide variety of boards currently using it, Policy Governance can work.

Does Separating Roles Restrict Communications?   Policy Governance boards make it clear that nobody's performance (board members' or staff members') will be evaluated against anything that has not been communicated in official board policy. With that safeguard firmly in place, all other forms of communication typically become freer than ever before. In any case, your board will use its policies to ensure that it is never left without the information and communication that it regards as essential to doing a good job. See pages 131–132 in Chapter Six.

Isn't Policy Governance Unnatural?   Things that flow from the way we see the world feel natural. If your board truly seeks to fulfill its job from the perspective of ownership and stops seeing it from the perspective of management, Policy Governance will soon come to feel natural. There is more discussion of this topic under the question "Can We Adapt the Policy Governance System?" later in this chapter.

Aren't We Already Doing It?   If your board can answer yes to all the following questions, you are. Otherwise, you are not.

1. Do you know who your owners are—legal as well as moral, if applicable?

2. Is everything you do connected to your owners collectively through your board's attitude, data, or personal interface with them?

3. Do you operate as the overall leadership—the first and last authority—within your organization?

4. Do you act as a *group* authority by speaking as one or not at all?

5. Do you have Ends (or alternatively named) policies that specify why your organization exists in terms of whose lives it will affect, what the impact will be, and the cost-efficiency with which that impact should be produced?

6. Do you have policies that specify your board's role and its conduct, as well as what you have delegated to whom and how their performance will be monitored and evaluated?

7. Do you have Executive Limitations (or alternatively named) policies that you can justify to your owners as *essential* ethical and prudential restrictions on the range of means choices that your CEO can make or allow?

8. In each category, are your policies designed from the top, covering every possible further topic at the broadest, most inclusive level first before progressively narrowing the range of possible interpretation until you have satisfied yourselves that you have said what you need to say?

9. Is your delegation of authority to the organization always clearly allocated—for example, to your CEO or equivalent?

10. Is your delegate free to make any reasonable interpretation of your Ends and Executive Limitations policies?

11. Is your chair or CGO free to make any reasonable interpretation of your policies for the board?

12. Do you regularly monitor and evaluate your CEO and yourselves against any reasonable interpretation of your policies?

Is Policy Governance a Commercial Product?   Anyone can use Policy Governance without any financial obligation to anyone. The ® after Policy Governance denotes that it is a registered service mark. The service mark is currently owned by John Carver and is maintained purely for the purpose of protecting the integrity of the principles and practices that make up the Policy Governance model.

Can We Adapt the Policy Governance System?   The answer to this question is yes, no, and yes. The first yes relates to the fact that no one can prevent you from using parts of the Policy Governance system rather than all of it. The no relates to the fact that unless you can answer yes to all twelve questions in the earlier list, you are not using the complete Policy Governance system as it was designed and therefore you cannot expect the results it was designed to produce (described on pages 9–12 in Chapter One). The second yes takes us back to the bike analogy, as follows:

You probably remember that once you really got the feel for riding your bike, you quickly became adept at wheelies, high-speed turns, and other tricks. You probably also remember that trying any of this before you had fully mastered the art of bike riding led to bruises and worse. Similarly, once your board members are truly coming from the perspective of ownership, they will be able to become extremely creative within the Policy Governance system because it will become obvious to them what does and does not fit with the principles that flow from ownership. However, tinkering with the system without being fully steeped in the ownership perspective almost inevitably damages your ability to govern for velocity.

How Flexible Is Policy Governance?   Policy Governance is very flexible in that it is a framework for putting *your* interpretation of your owners' values into action. It does not tell your board what to think, only how to organize how it thinks in order to be productive. In addition, there are many adaptations that can be made to the Policy Governance system that do no harm because they do not change any component part in a manner that defeats its purpose. Throughout this book, I will be providing examples of such adaptations.

Is Policy Governance Safe?   Ultimately, risk—financial, legal, or any other sort—cannot be entirely avoided. When one is riding a bike, all the safeguards and precautions and insurances in the world cannot prevent a freak accident. Whatever we do in our lives, some degree of risk is inevitable. Boards cannot avoid risk; they can only manage it as intelligently as they are able.

As Chapter Eight details, the Policy Governance system enables boards to *verifiably demonstrate* that

- They have anticipated *all* actual and potential risks, known and unknown.
- Those risks are governed through a set of policy controls that encompass all the organization's affairs.
- They regularly monitor organizational compliance with each control in a manner that requires full disclosure of interpretation and data.

Endorsement of Policy Governance by legal counsels of boards across the world; its direct use by a variety of law societies, accounting bodies, and judicial bodies; and the encouragement of eminent organizations such as BP plc and eminent persons such as Sir Adrian Cadbury support the view of Hugh Kelly QC, associate counsel at Miller Thomson LLP: "The board of a Canadian charitable corporation that adopts Policy Governance® has performed 'due diligence,' and fulfilled all legal obligations imposed upon its directors. On a comparative basis, such boards and directors are far ahead of most corporations, even those in the world of commerce, in observing their legal and moral obligations" (Kelly, 2003).

Is There Research That Proves That Policy Governance Works? Governance research generally is in its infancy. While no real research exists, there is increasing evidence in the business world that when boards become more aware of their owners, as Policy Governance requires, better company performance results. It would seem reasonable to expect that similar results would flow from increased owner focus in other sectors, but to date we have no research to verify that expectation.

Researchers who have attempted to compare the effectiveness of different governance approaches inevitably start with some assumptions about what effective governance should produce. Typically, these assumptions fall into the following categories:

- Effective boards = happy or satisfied board members.
- Effective boards = richer or financially successful organizations.
- Effective boards = busier or more productive organizations.
- Effective boards = the demands of regulators being met.

From a Policy Governance perspective, however, the criterion for judging the effectiveness of governance does not lie in any of the preceding categories per se but in the conversion of "a judicious summary of owners' intentions into organizational performance" (Carver, 2006, p. 339). The distinction is critical, for an organization with happy board members and increasing amounts of funding and programs and a great record of regulatory compliance could still be failing according to the Policy Governance criterion, and vice versa. Happy board members, increasing amounts of funding and programs, or a great record of regulatory compliance do not necessarily tell us that the organization is accomplishing its purpose or operating in tune with its owners' values.

To further illustrate the point, let's take the issue of an organization's financial health. It would be perfectly possible to have a for-profit corporation generating huge profits but incurring a level of risk that its owners would regard as totally unacceptable. Similarly, one could imagine a nonprofit that has had some pretty dire financial results for a couple of years but only because it turned down a grant that came with unacceptable strings. Thus, the measures that some people are using to judge the impact of boards on organizational performance can only be indicators—and very crude ones, at that.

In any case, from a Policy Governance perspective, we are asking the wrong people when we measure organizational performance based on the opinion of CEOs, board members, chairs, or CGOs or their consultants, for Policy Governance is based on the principle that ultimately, only owners have the legitimate right to say what performance is.

For a useful overview of current research on Policy Governance, see Hough, McGregor-Lowndes, and Ryan, 2004. For a more detailed critique of the state of current research on governance in general and Policy Governance in particular, see Chapter Twelve of the third edition of *Boards That Make a Difference* by John Carver (2006).

CONFIRMING WHAT YOUR BOARD HAS LEARNED

A final and crucial step in framing your decision-making discussion is to review what has been learned and confirm the learning. It is vital to make sure that everyone is clear about what the board has learned about Policy Governance and how they see themselves and their future as a board.

Here are a couple of ideas that might be useful for helping your board to summarize the results of its Policy Governance learning process. Forced-association techniques are easy to set up and, in my experience, help to create a good atmosphere for free exchange. For example, take a bag of small objects or a selection of pictures from a magazine and ask people to speak to why the object reminds them of governance or Policy Governance. Or give each person one prompt such as "What I have learned is . . . ," "What I still don't know is . . . ," "What I think we should do now is . . . ," "I think we are ready for . . . ," or "I hope we . . . ." Then have everyone move around the room, ask everyone else the question, write all the answers down, and be ready to report to the whole group.

One of the biggest things that I have learned from the experience of working with boards of all sorts is that you should never assume that you know what your fellow board members are thinking. Time and again, I have looked at a group and thought that they were not at all interested in change, only to find upon doing a summarizing exercise that everyone is inspired and ready to go! A more detailed process for helping your board summarize what it has learned and begin the work of coming to a decision is outlined in Tool 2.8 at the end of the chapter.

MAKING UP YOUR MINDS

Having learned about Policy Governance and considered the pros and cons for your board, you now need to decide whether you are going to move forward to the next stage—putting your policies in place. This is a big step, for although you are not absolutely committed until you have taken a formal vote to enact your first set of policies, getting to that point will require a substantial investment. The reality is that very few boards that go to the next stage turn back afterward. Thus, this is a critical moment of decision.

While boards do not usually require unanimity for decisions to be made, they do typically strive for a good level of mutual understanding of the issues such that board members who find themselves in the minority don't find it too hard to respect the official outcome. And for a decision as important as adopting a new system for doing your governing job, it is certainly not a good idea to go ahead with less than a significant majority.

Good board process is not only about ensuring that everyone is heard; it is also about organizing the discussion so that it moves the group from exploration to a well-justified conclusion. A well-justified conclusion is one that has been reached in a manner that everyone can support, even if the outcome is not what they were hoping for.

Voting to Move Forward

Once your deliberation process has been completed, you will need to take and record a vote on whether to move to the next step. Here is a suggestion for appropriate wording for the motion: "Having thoroughly investigated various approaches to job design for boards, this board is resolved to codify its values using the Policy Governance system in preparation for making a final decision on adopting that system."

Dealing with Dissent

If your board has gone through the research and decision-making process in a thorough and respectful manner, it is highly likely that even those who are not entirely comfortable with a vote to move to Policy Governance will feel that they should not stand in the way but rather should support the majority decision. There are no guarantees, however.

Should you find yourselves completely divided, of course, you will need to at least postpone the decision. My suggestion is that before dropping the subject, you all agree on a time—say, a couple of years hence—at which the board will reevaluate its current approach as well as other possible approaches as part of a whole-board commitment to continuous improvement.

If, on the other hand, you are dealing with an individual dissenter or a small minority of dissenters and the majority of board members are raring to go, the board needs to consider its options very carefully. Options might include

- Asking the dissenting board member (or members) what they would need in order to feel comfortable with going ahead (for example, a commitment to evaluate the board's progress after a certain amount of time)
- Asking the dissenting board member (or members) whether they would consider withdrawing in favor of new board members who are committed to operating in the way that the majority of the board would like to operate
- Providing further education, such as the opportunity to meet other boards that are using Policy Governance

MOVING ON

The next chapters provide valuable information to further your research on Policy Governance, including information about the installation process. In particular, Chapter Eight will help you take into consideration your people, your circumstances, and all the planning you need to do to make your transition successful. Even if your board decides that it does not want to implement Policy Governance, you should find some of the ideas in the following chapters a useful complement to your practice.

TOOLS

 ## TOOL 2.1 DECISION-MAKING PROCESS

1. Full board refines the substantive question or questions it is trying to answer—for example,

   a. Should this board adopt a more systematic approach to governance?

   b. Should this board move to a system based on policy controls?

   c. Should this board adopt the Policy Governance system?

2. Full board agrees on key elements of decision-making process, including target completion date, research and information required, and voting threshold (for example, majority vote, two-thirds majority, whole board) required for final conclusion.

   a. Full board deputizes person or persons to create detailed action plan and timetable based on the requirements just listed.

3. Full board meets to review information gathered as a result of item 2 and discuss questions such as

   a. On whose behalf are we making this decision?

   b. What could we gain?

   c. What could we lose?

   d. What would it cost to change?

   e. What would it cost to stay as we are?

f. Is governance an art or a science?

g. Can you have accountability without freedom?

4. Straw poll to test the water on substantive question or questions agreed on in item 1. Full board agrees on the form and content of any further information they require, if any, before taking a final vote—for example,

a. Further reading

b. Video

c. Telephone interviews with Policy Governance users

d. Attendance at a Policy Governance workshop

e. Formal full board introduction from a Policy Governance consultant

5. Full board votes.

TOOL 2.2 OUR CURRENT GOVERNANCE ASSUMPTIONS: A QUESTIONNAIRE

Rank your response on a scale from 1 to 10 in which 1 is "completely disagree" and 10 is "completely agree."

1. Boards exist to ensure that things don't go wrong. _____

2. Boards exist to define the future. _____

3. Boards need to know all about what goes on inside their organization. _____

4. Boards need to know about what's going on in the outside world that may affect their organization. _____

5. Boards need to control. _____

6. Boards need to empower. _____

7. Boards need to coach. _____

8. Boards are very important. _____

TOOL 2.3 LEARNING STYLES AND PATHWAYS

The following descriptions of learning styles are based on the work of Barbara A. Soloman and Richard M. Felder, both of North Carolina State University in Raleigh. A full description of the styles is available at http://www4.ncsu.edu/unity/lockers/users/f/felder/public/ILSdir/styles.htm.

A free online questionnaire that can be used to identify your own learning style can be found at http://www.engr.ncsu.edu/learningstyles/ilsweb.html.

LEARNING STYLE	DESCRIPTION	SAMPLE LEARNING RESOURCES
Active	Tends to retain and understand information best by doing something active with it—discussing it, applying it, or explaining it to others	Governance rehearsal. See p. 206 in Resources section. Trial of Miss Polly C. See p. 23. What ifs. See p. 128 in Chapter Six.
Reflective	Prefers to think about things quietly first	Books. See Resources section.
Sensing	Tends to like learning facts and solving problems through well-established methods	Books. See Resources section. Inquiry tools. See Chapter Two.
Intuitive	Often prefers discovering possibilities and relationships	Cafés. See Resources Section.
Visual	Remembers best what they see—for example, pictures, diagrams, flowcharts, timelines, films, and demonstrations	Videos. See Resources Section. Visual analogies. Picture association. See p. 30 in Chapter Two.
Verbal	Gets more out of words—for example, written and spoken explanations	Videos. See Resources Section. Online learning. See Resources Section. In-person presentations. See p. 181 in Chapter 8.
Sequential	Tends to gain understanding in linear steps in which each step follows logically from the previous one	Reading. See Resources Section. Logical explanations—for example, PowerPoint presentations

| Global | Tends to learn in large jumps, absorbing material almost randomly without seeing connections and then suddenly "getting it" | A combination of the resources listed in this column for the other learning styles |

TOOL 2.4 WHAT DO YOU WANT TO ACHIEVE AS A BOARD?

Step One: Where Are You Now?

Ask individual board members to complete a series of open-ended statements such as

1. Our board is ultimately accountable to . . .

2. Our connection with those to whom we are ultimately accountable is . . .

3. Our directions to our CEO are . . .

4. Our evaluation of our CEO is . . .

5. The way we organize and conduct ourselves as a board is . . .

6. Our evaluation of ourselves as a board is . . .

7. The most important thing for our board now is . . .

Feed the answers back to the whole board. Ask the board to discuss and summarize what their answers reveal about where the board is today. Note key points on a flipchart.

Step Two: Your Goals for Governance

Ask board members to discuss what goals they might set for themselves, based on the discussion in Step One. Note these on a flipchart. Confirm that these goals are the criteria that the board would wish to use in assessing the merits of a governance system or methodology.

TOOL 2.5 APPROXIMATE TIME AND MONEY COSTS INVOLVED IN INTRODUCING POLICY GOVERNANCE

ITEM	BOARD TIME	CEO TIME	FINANCE
Initial research and consideration	At least six hours, allowing time for two or more significant discussions plus any reading and research assignments	At least six hours, allowing time for two or more significant discussions plus any reading and research assignments	Recommended: Cost of trained Policy Governance consultant for one-day introduction
Means policy development	At least two days, to follow as rapidly as possible from initial research and consideration	At least two days with board plus time to undertake review with wider staff	Recommended: Cost of trained Policy Governance consultant to facilitate policy development sessions
Ends policy development	At least one and a half days including time for research; can be scheduled whenever suits the board	At least two days, allowing for time to undertake review with wider staff	Recommended: Cost of trained Policy Governance consultant to facilitate policy development sessions
Board planning	At least three hours to establish annual calendar (including ownership linkage and board education and support plans) and policy monitoring and board and CEO evaluation schedule	At least three hours with board	Recommended: Cost of trained Policy Governance consultant to facilitate planning sessions
Monitoring training	At least two hours	At least half a day for CEO and key delegates	Recommended: Cost of trained Policy Governance consultant to facilitate monitoring training

The following questionnaire is designed to help your board consider the cost of continuing without Policy Governance. The questionnaire could be completed individually before or during a meeting at which the results are discussed, or it could simply be used as a guide to topics for a full board discussion.

1. Are we clear on what it means when we have approved something?

   a. It means that we have fully understood it, considered it, and taken direct responsibility for it.

   b. It means that we have simply acknowledged that we have seen it, and no more.

   c. It means that we expect to be asked to re-approve it if there are any future changes to what we have just approved.

   d. Not sure what it means

   e. Other (please specify)

2. Are we being asked to make judgments on things that we have little or no knowledge of?

   a. All the time

   b. Much of the time

   c. Some of the time

   d. Rarely

   e. Never

3. Do we know why we are making judgments about some things and not others?

   a. Yes

   b. No

4. When we approve something that was brought to us by the CEO and it turns out to be a mistake, whom does accountability rest with?

   a. The board entirely

   b. The CEO entirely

c. Both the board and the CEO, to some degree

d. No one

5. Have we established criteria for our own and our CEO's decision making?

    a. Yes

    b. No

6. What are the consequences, if any, of the above?

 ## TOOL 2.7 GETTING CONCERNS ON THE TABLE

Ask every board member to write down their responses to the following prompts either before or during the relevant board meeting. Let them know that they need to write clearly because someone else may be reading their words out loud. Also let them know that there are no right answers and that brief "top of mind" responses are all that are sought.

- The thing I would like to raise but feel I can't is . . .
- My biggest fear about this is . . .
- The questions I have are . . .
- And the other thing I would like to say is . . .

Feed the answers back to the whole board anonymously. Ask the board to discuss and summarize what their answers reveal about where the board is today. Note key points on a flipchart, group them, and rank them according to how important they seem to be.

Finally, ask every board member to write down their responses to the following prompts:

- As a result of this exercise, I see . . .
- As a result of this exercise, I feel . . .
- What we need to do now is . . .

Feed the answers back to the whole board, and then create an action plan that details how and when you will discuss the outstanding questions and concerns.

TOOL 2.8 OBJECTIVE, REFLECTIVE, INTERPRETIVE, AND DECISIONAL DISCUSSION METHOD

Use this discussion method after your board has finished a thorough review of Policy Governance. You can use the questions to facilitate an informal whole-group discussion (be sure to give people plenty of time to think about the questions) or assign the questions as individual work that then gets shared anonymously and only then discussed with the whole group.

1. Objective discussion: drawing out the facts. Ask questions like these:
   - What are the main principles of Policy Governance?
   - What does practicing Policy Governance require?
   - What are the main benefits of Policy Governance?
   - What are the main costs associated with Policy Governance?

2. Reflective discussion: drawing out how your board feels about its exploration
   - How do you feel about our learning process?
   - What was the biggest learning for you?
   - What was the biggest challenge for you?
   - How do you feel about where we are now?

3. Interpretive discussion: enabling your board to consider the meaning and value of its learning
   - What have we achieved in this process?
   - What would we say about it to someone who was not here?
   - Why were we willing to take this on in the first place?

- If we were to be able to do this again, what would we change? Keep the same?

4. Decisional discussion: enabling the group to make a decision or respond to the experience

   - Would using the Policy Governance system help us to achieve our goals for governance?

   - What would it take for us to use Policy Governance?

   - Are we prepared to do what it would take?

   - Shall we proceed to developing our first draft policy set?

Knowing Who Owns Your Organization

*Discovery consists of seeing what everybody has seen,
and thinking what nobody has thought.*

Albert Szent-Gyorgi

Getting started with Policy Governance requires, more than anything else, a profound understanding of governance as responsible ownership. Inspired by this understanding, your board will find organizing itself through Policy Governance both exciting and natural. Without this understanding, you may well find everything a struggle.

The origins of Policy Governance lie in John Carver's search to understand the role of boards. What he came up with is the theory that the role of a board is to act as the ownership of their organization as well as a methodology for making that theory count in practice. The theory of the board as the owners' representative will not sound like news to many readers of this book, and indeed, at a superficial level, it isn't. What is new, however, is the use of that theory as an organizing principle that lies behind a systematic approach to the work of any board. This chapter explores the theory of the board as owners' representative and how the Policy Governance system flows directly from it.

Once you have read this chapter, you should be in a position to understand

- The relationship between board governance and ownership
- What establishing an ownership connection means for your organization
- Why having an ownership connection is required in order to implement Policy Governance

OWNERSHIP: THE SOURCE OF A BOARD'S AUTHORITY

When an organization is incorporated either as a for-profit or a nonprofit entity, it becomes a legal person and thus gains certain protections in law. The authority to incorporate is given by the societies in which we live and is subject to each corporation's compliance with the law and the terms of their founding document—a certificate of incorporation, a corporate charter, articles of incorporation, or the equivalent.

Having established their authority, the owners of the corporation need to ensure that their organization is governed. Typically, they do this by, in effect, delegating their authority to a board within any reasonable interpretation of their founding documentation, their bylaws, or any shareholder agreements. Finally, most boards find that they need to give a considerable amount of their authority to people whom they employ to get things done—people whom we shall refer to as *staff*.

To summarize, the staff has no authority that does not come from the board; boards have no authority that does not come from owners; and in democracies, at least, owners have no authority that is not sanctioned by all citizens through their relevant legislators and regulators.

MINE TO OURS: THE RIGHTS AND RESPONSIBILITIES OF OWNERSHIP

We know that ownership affects us all the time in many different ways, but what does it really mean? I own my car; it is mine. We own our world; it is ours. These are two enormously different ownership contexts. Yet whether we talk about ownership of assets in a personal or collective sense, in a legal or moral sense, there are some vital commonalities.

If you own something, be it a house or a school system, subject only to the law, you have the right to do whatever you want with it, which generally includes the right to neglect it, abandon it, or destroy it. However if you do neglect, abandon, or destroy what you own, its value to you will be lost. Thus, you will usually take one of these courses only if you believe that your asset has become more of a liability than an investment.

In all other cases, if you own something, you will care for it for yourself *and for all possible future owners,* for that is the only way in which you will be able to preserve and even, you may hope, enhance your investment. In other words, even if you intend to sell the item or give it away tomorrow or hold onto it for your entire life, you have to look after it on behalf of other people—people who might want to buy it, lease it, inherit it, or otherwise acquire it—or you will lose its value. In other words, when we are talking about owning assets, their value can only be protected and enhanced if it is transferable to others.

Ultimately, therefore, ownership cannot be entirely self-centered. If I don't look after my things as if they were ours and if I don't look after our things as if they were mine, I will be left with nothing. It is in this sense that your board's role is to act as the ownership of your organization. It is in this sense that owners' best interests and the organization's best interests are synonymous. If I abuse the company I own, if I don't repair the roof of my house, if I don't change the oil in my car, if I don't care for the planet, I will lose my ability to realize their value. The best interests of my company, my house, my car, and my planet are, ultimately, my best interests.

If you are the responsible owner of an asset, you will

- Care for its value beyond your own personal use of it
- Be concerned with it as a whole
- Want it to be productive
- Want it to be safe

If you are to be a Policy Governance board, you need to start from here.

WHO ARE YOUR LEGAL AND MORAL OWNERS?

This may seem a strange thing to say, but if you agree with the theory that your board's role is to act as the ownership of your organization, it follows that being on a board is not about you as an individual. Stated another way, you are not there to be you; you are there to be the ownership, whoever they may be. So your first order of business is to find out who your owners are. Policy Governance asks you to consider two kinds of ownership: legal and moral.

Legal Ownership

The first place you can look to find out the identity of your ownership is your bylaws or other founding documents. Whoever has the right to hire and fire your board at your organization's annual meeting—those people are your legal owners.

Over time, your board may be able to have considerable influence in shaping your organization's legal ownership. For example, the board of a privately held equity corporation can, with the agreement of the current shareholders, choose to go public, to issue certain classes of shares, or to merge with another corporation. In another example, the board of an association can, with the agreement of the current legal ownership (usually synonymous with the association's membership), choose to merge with another association. And the board of a charity whose legal ownership as set out in their bylaws consists entirely of the current board members (as is often the case) can select whomever they choose to join them. But on any given day, the important thing to know is that your board has no choice but to be accountable to your organization's legal owners for everything your organization is and does.

To make the point even more strongly, boards that treat their legal owners lightly are putting themselves and their organization in grave danger. Legal owners have serious powers, including, ultimately, the power to dissolve your organization entirely if they don't like the way things are going.

Moral Ownership

Subject only to your legal owners' ultimate right to veto anything your board does, your board can also choose to consider itself accountable to a wider group of moral owners. This particularly makes sense for nonprofit boards that are self-appointing, but it can make sense for many others, too. For, while identifying a moral ownership is not a requirement, every board needs to recognize that if it cannot create a sense of ownership beyond current board members and legal owners, their board and, therefore, their organization will ultimately become unsustainable.

Whatever you decide, you will need to choose very wisely, for your interpretation of your owners' best interests will dictate almost everything you do.

Non-Owner Interests

Because owners are your board's touchstone for everything it does, it is important not to confuse owners with other stakeholders such as customers (whom your organization may think of as clients, consumers, users, or patients, for example), staff, or suppliers. Much as these people certainly have a vested interest in your organization's success, unless they share the ownership motivation, their interests do not meet the ownership motivation test. In other words, unless they care for the value of your organization beyond its ability to meet their own personal needs and desires, treating them as owners will take you down the wrong track.

For example, the board of a hospital will have concerns about patients with many different conditions, who would all like the board to make sure that more of the hospital's resources go toward meeting their needs. That same board will also have to consider individual employee groups and significant suppliers of equipment and drugs, who would all like the board to make sure that the services or goods that they provide are properly recognized. The problem, of course, is that if the board were to ensure that everyone got what they wanted, in a very short space of time, there would be nothing left of anything for anyone. So in the context of a hospital, it is vital that the board take its cue from the right people—its ownership—which, in this case, is likely to be members of the community who care about the long-term viability of the hospital as a resource for the whole community's health.

Clarifying Your Organization's Ownership

Becoming and staying clear about your ownership is not always easy. Yet in principle, before your board can commit to making any other decisions, it needs to decide on whose behalf it will make all its decisions. Most important, your board needs to know who its owners are before it can decide what your organization's reason for existence is and therefore what its Ends are. Successful installation of the Policy Governance system is thus dependent on identifying your ownership. For while there are many people and organizations—legislators, regulators, professional associations, trade unions, and the like—who rightfully should have a say in how your organization behaves, only owners can legitimately claim to be the ultimate decision makers about the three Ends questions of what benefit your organization exists to produce, for whom, and with what cost-efficiency.

To illustrate the point, an organization that exists to raise charitable funds within a local community could, among other choices, answer the questions as to whom it seeks to benefit by stating any of the following:

- Those who wish to donate funds to local causes

- Disadvantaged persons in the community

- Organizations that deliver services to disadvantaged persons in the community

Clearly, each of these conclusions would give rise to the creation of a very different organization, so which is the "right" one? The answer is that without knowing who the ownership is and what their motivations are, we cannot say. In other words, we have to know who the owners are and what their motivations are before we can decide whom the organization should be benefiting and therefore know what the right kind of organization would be.

Determining ownership is a lot easier for some organizations than others. The following sections discuss some common situations and issues that give rise to confusion about ownership.

Ownership and Self-Appointing Boards   If you are a member of a board that is self-appointing, you may have a bewildering array of choices about who your owners might be. For example, if your organization deals with youth, your owners could be parents in your community, young people themselves, potential employers, the community as a whole, youth leaders, or any combination thereof. And because you are the legal owners, the decision is entirely yours.

One way to approach this decision is to look at yourselves as board members. Who are you? What has been so compelling to you and your board's founders and predecessors that you have given up your time to sit on this board? Whatever it is that inspired you to join the board and continue to be involved is likely to be an ownership motivation. And maybe understanding who you are and your own motivation will enable you to find more people like you—more owners.

Ownership and Closely Held Boards   Some boards are entirely or almost entirely appointed by a superior body such as a branch of government or a holding company board or other majority owner. Tightening their hold over your board further, such superior bodies or persons may choose to impose shareholder agreements. These agreements act in place of or like an extension of your board's bylaws and can give the legal owners all sorts of rights—for example, the right to veto the hiring, firing, or compensation of your CEO. If your board is in this situation, you may well wonder why your owners bothered setting up the board in the first place if they were going to circumscribe your decisions and actions so tightly. Yet you do have a choice. Either you can settle for being little more than an owner-CEO go-between, or you can try to negotiate with your owners for more freedom by impressing upon them that (1) there is little job satisfaction in playing such a passive part, so keeping board members will be difficult, and (2) in the event of future problems, their board and their organization would be better protected if the board could show that it had provided more than a fig leaf of decency.

Ownership and Public Sector Boards   Governments that wish to relinquish some of their responsibilities will often create new organizations to take over some of their work. Often, such a new organization has its own board and, apparently, its own independent direct accountability to the community (whether a local, national, or specific interest community). However, the government department concerned is often extremely fearful that the devolution might come back to haunt it if the new board fails. This fear often leads government to impose such stringent controls that the new board is left highly uncertain about who its real owners are. If your board is in such a situation, it may have to make a choice: (1) to consider itself an arm of government and seek to ensure that the government lives up to its ownership responsibilities, including sensible delegation, or (2) to consider itself independently owned by its community and treat compliance with the government-imposed controls as merely the cost of doing business.

Ownership and Customers   Particularly in the nonprofit and public sectors, it is very common for boards to be dominated by customer (or beneficiary) rather than ownership interests. As I discussed earlier in this chapter, there are real dangers when a board extrapolates up from consumer values rather than down from owner values. For management, the importance of putting the interests of customers—whether they are patients, students, or other consumers—first is obvious. For management, customer satisfaction is critical to success. But in the boardroom, the first question must be "On behalf of our owners, which needs of which customers or potential customers do we exist to satisfy?"

In some cases, of course, customers are owners, too. Examples include the members of associations, cooperatives, and credit unions as well as the shareholders of companies that are deliberately setting out to create "investomers." In all these cases, the principle of the board's need to operate from the interests of owners remains. The fact that distinguishing those interests is more challenging does not make doing so any less important.

Ownership and Funders   In for-profit corporations, being a financial investor automatically makes you a legal owner and therefore someone to whom the board is legally accountable. Of course, there are some types of investors, such as day traders, who have little or no real ownership interest, a fact that the board must bear in mind when it comes to weighing their relative influence on its thinking. Neither does being a lender such as a bank automatically make you an owner unless your interest in an organization goes beyond ensuring that its contract with your bank is fulfilled.

The same goes for funders in the nonprofit sector. Funders who are so committed to the long-term health of your organization that they donate money to your core costs are probably owners, but funders who give you money only to do the things that they want done are more like contractors for a service than owners. Owners, as John Carver has said, are not the people or organizations with whom the board makes a deal but those whom the board has no moral right not to recognize (Carver, 2006, p. 188).

Ownership, Management, and Staff   A large part of the job of acting as the ownership of an organization is directing and monitoring the management of the organization, usually through a CEO. When staff are also owners, as in the case of worker cooperatives and companies that give their staff shares, and particularly when staff are given seats on the board, as in the case of many corporate and some public sector boards, several potential conflicts of interest immediately arise. How can a manager also be an evaluator of management performance? How can a manager also be a determiner of management compensation? How can a manager participate in any decision in which the best interests of owners and the best interests of staff might be at odds? What happens to a CEO's authority and ability to hold other managers accountable when they are also fellow board members? With a lot of forethought and effort, such conflicts can be managed, but it is usually preferable to avoid them altogether by keeping managers off the board.

If you are using the Policy Governance system, you do not need managers on the board in order to be informed or to keep your CEO honest. Policy Governance policy controls and monitoring can be used to ensure that you get all the independent information you need, as can be seen on pages 131–132 of Chapter Seven. If you have no option other than to have managers on your board, you need to distinguish all the actual and potential conflicts of interest that they could face and then create policies in your Governance Process category that require them to absent themselves from discussion of the relevant matters, as referred to on page 168 in Chapter Eight.

Some boards, especially founding boards, consist entirely of people who also run the organization, whether as entrepreneurs, volunteers, or employees. These board members are truly the wearers of many hats—owner, board member, manager, staff member, and maybe even customer, too. Keeping roles separate is a challenge but can make a huge difference for all concerned. For example, if you are an entrepreneur who minds your own shop, the chances of expanding your business are likely to be much higher if you think about your role as owner separately from your role as worker. And if you are a volunteer parent in an after-school program (and therefore both a worker and a customer), your potential impact over the long term will be far greater if you separate your interests as a parent and a volunteer from your interest at the broader ownership level on behalf of all current and future parents, volunteers, and students and put yourself forward as a board member.

A Note on Advisory Boards   Advisory boards have no power to direct or control and are not boards in the sense of being accountable to owners for the success and safety of their organization. Therefore, they do not fall into the category of governing boards, which are the subject of this book.

As can be seen from all the situations described earlier in this chapter, clarifying your ownership as part of introducing Policy Governance can involve your board in some very important decisions. And it doesn't stop there. Having clarified your organization's ownership, your board needs to determine how it is going to conduct its relationship with its owners, which means that it needs to distinguish what it means to be an owner's representative.

BEING OWNERS' REPRESENTATIVE

As we have seen in some of the preceding cases, even when distinguishing your owners is straightforward, you still may have to take into account that they are not necessarily infused with the spirit of responsible ownership. Some owners are utterly irresponsible—that is, they do not care for your organization beyond their own personal use of it, are not concerned with it as a whole, and do not care whether it is productive or safe. And as long as they are acting within the laws of their land, they have every right to be so.

Day traders care about the value of the companies they invest in but usually only from a very short-term perspective. Parents care about the local schools into which their taxes go, but typically not much beyond the moment when their child heads off to work or further education. Clearly, all of these owners are acting well within their legal rights. However, a board has to remember that when owners legally or morally appoint them, they are in effect outsourcing their ownership to them. And as owners' representative, unless the board is directly told otherwise, it has no option other than to assume that its owners wish it to play that role responsibly. Thus, from a legal as well as a moral perspective, although owners themselves can do anything they want with their own assets, boards acting on their behalf cannot deliberately harm their assets nor change their ownership without the current owners' permission.

Protecting Owners from Themselves

In effect, boards are charged with being more owner-like than most owners are themselves. The actual owners may for the most part be so passive as to be invisible, or completely unaware that they are owners, or prone to such shortsighted behavior that they threaten the survival of their own asset. None of these conditions make a difference in the board's responsibility to act as a responsible owner on their behalf.

For example, when owners try to use their ownership authority to force their individual interests as customers, the board needs to be ready to defend themselves and their CEO. It is the board's responsibility to be the link between owners and their organization, and the board that leaves its CEO at the mercy of owners who do not realize that they are shooting themselves in the foot is a board that is not doing its job. For example, when board members who are responsible for a number of public schools in a given community fail to defend a CEO's decision to close a particular school that has been made in the best interests of fulfilling the Ends that they, the school board, have developed on behalf of the ownership of the school system, they are not only letting their CEO and themselves down but shortchanging the owners as a whole.

Being owners' representative, therefore, is not about being a mere messenger between owners and managers, nor is it about representing any subset of owners. It is about standing in for or acting on behalf of the ownership as a whole, taking an informed view of their best interests. The responsible board member is one who might say, "I vote the way my owners would vote if they

- Knew what I know
- Had a future perspective
- Had an obligation to represent *all* owners"

Weighing Different Owners' Interests

One of the biggest challenges that boards face in acting on behalf of the ownership as a whole is balancing the best interests of different groups of owners. In the sections that follow, I will briefly touch on some of the issues involved in relation to a couple of important subsets of ownership.

Minority Owners   Even in for-profit corporations, in which minority owners have specific legal rights, boards are left with many difficult issues to address in relation to minority owners. For example, think again of a local education authority. How far should they take account of the fact that a minority of their local taxpayer owners speak a different language or practice a different religion in determining what the school system in their area should be producing and for whom? Boards are always going to have to consider subsets of the ownership, some of whom may create problems for the majority if they believe that they are not being paid sufficient attention. Unhappy minority owners represent a risk to majority shareholders—a risk that the board must manage.

Being prepared is the key. The only way that your board can defend itself is by being very clear about the profile of its entire ownership and setting up good processes for gathering and discussing ownership input that ensure that minority voices are fully heard. Minority owners may still not be satisfied with your decisions, but at least the arguments over process can be minimized. And sometimes you may be able to help minority owners to frame their concern in a manner that speaks to the best interests of all owners, thus helping them make their point with much greater force.

Potential Future Owners   In considering your definition of your organization's ownership, your board may also want to consider the degree to which it wants to take into account the interests of future owners. To say that boards are only obliged to concern themselves with the interests of today's owners is not necessarily as black-and-white a statement as it may seem. For example, as the board of a publicly listed company, how should you balance the harm that might be done to the value of your current shareholders' stock as a result of disclosing a possible risk against the harm that might be done to your current *and* future shareholders by not disclosing that same risk? And how can a board prevent owner-executives with significant shares from taking huge risks, ostensibly in an effort to benefit today's shareholders but ultimately damaging all shareholders' best interests, including their own? And what about boards that use poison pills to deter takeovers by potential future shareholders? Are they really protecting the interests of current shareholders by keeping future shareholders out? Or are they protecting the interests of corporate executives at the expense of their current shareholders' right to sell their shares to the highest bidder?

In the nonprofit arena, too, it can make sense for a board to broaden its definition of its current ownership to take some account of the interests of future owners. For example, boards of associations might well be advised to treat potential association members as part of their moral ownership, in part to protect themselves from being held hostage by members who are operating from a customer's motivation rather than an owner's motivation. In any case, your board might think it worthwhile to consider how matters such as its level of tolerance for risk are likely to be affected by its attitude toward the interests of future shareholders.

KNOWING WHAT YOUR OWNERS WANT FROM YOU

Once you have identified the composition of your ownership and how you are going to weight the interests of relevant subgroups within it, you have created the most critical reference point for development of all your policies, including your Ends policies. Now the challenge is interpreting what your owners want from you.

Boards use owners' capital to do their work, whether it is in the form of cash and authority or just authority. Legal owners' ultimate sanction is to withdraw that capital, so it is important that the board take full account of legal owners' wishes and that the board feel that it can always justify its decisions as being in the best interests of all owners, including minority owners. Moral owners can also withdraw their support in whatever form it has been given and thereby cause great difficulty for all involved. In any case, if your board and your organization are failing to act in accordance with your owners' wishes, you are not only failing to fulfill your ultimate purpose, you are putting your board and your organization in jeopardy.

So what do your organization's owners want from you? Indeed, what do any organization's owners want?

Success

Briefly stated, what owners of all types of organizations want is shareholder value. Of course, what owners consider to be value differs drastically, but the important thing is that it is considered to be value. In other words, what owners want is some good for some people. It could be housing for the homeless, food for the hungry, or a financial return on their hard-earned money for themselves and their families; the possibilities are endless. Your constitutional document and bylaws will state the arena in which the value is to be generated in some sort of statement of purpose; however, that statement will usually leave many specifics unanswered.

Who are your owners seeking to benefit? What priority would they want to give to particular subgroups of those beneficiaries, if any? How would your owners like those beneficiaries' lives to be different as a result of your organization's efforts? These are the kinds of questions your board needs to be asking if it is going to hold itself accountable to your owners for the interpretation and pursuit of their interests. All of these questions about the definition of success—the answers to which become, in Policy Governance terms, your Ends—will be detailed much more fully in Chapter Five.

Safe and Ethical Operation

Your owners rely on their asset—your organization—to produce the value they desire. Thus, they want their board to use that asset in a manner that does not exceed their appetite for risk nor breach their ethical standards. In this way, the board's relationship with its ownership provides not only its ultimate direction in terms of the value it exists to produce but also a barometer for its attitude toward risk as well as its moral compass. These questions of safety and ethics will be addressed in much more detail in Chapter Six.

A Great Board

Your owners would like you to be a great board, which, very broadly speaking, means that they want you to produce value in a safe and ethical manner. But there are other components involved in being a great board that you might reasonably expect owners to cite; some of these are outlined in the following list:

Characteristics That Owners Might Expect of a Great Board

Uncompromising in its allegiance to owners' interests. Board members should be as free from conflicts of interest as possible. Boards should have clear processes to ensure that any unavoidable conflicts are declared and then managed effectively.

Focused on the best interests of all owners. Boards should strive to ensure that they can justify everything they do as being in the best interests of all owners (including, to an appropriate degree, the best interests of future owners). Board members should not pursue the interests of any subset of owners to the exclusion of other owners.

Able to ensure successful, safe, and ethical operation. Boards should be able to assure their owners that their organization is delivering a reasonable interpretation of their best interests in terms of a successful, safe, and ethical operation.

Disciplined enough to act as a group authority. Owners' authority lies in the board as a whole and not in any one board member. Even if your board members were appointed or elected as individuals, they were all appointed or elected to govern everything on behalf of everyone. Thus, owners need their board members to be disciplined enough to act as a principled group authority rather than as individual players in a personality-driven combat zone.

Diverse enough to make wise decisions. Wise decisions are decisions that have been arrived at through examining multiple viewpoints. Owners expect boards to bring to bear a variety of opinions and outlooks that reflect their own diversity.

Willing to get independent expert help when needed. Owners need boards to be humble enough to know what they don't know, realistic enough to know that they can never know everything, and willing to get the advice they need when they need it.

In command. Owners need boards to be leaders, not followers—that is, clearly in charge, providing proactive leadership that transcends the executives of the month. Owners need boards to be clear and firm about what their expectations are and who has what authority.

In communication. Owners need boards to use regular communication with them to create the organization's future and be accountable.

Aware of the value of their own role. Owners need boards to value their role as ownership representatives and invest in the education and administrative resources needed for good performance.

The preceding section is a brief and general overview of what your owners are likely to want from you. Clearly, you need to get more specific, and to do that, you are going to have to engage your owners in some sort of dialogue.

BUILDING OWNER RELATIONS

For-profit corporations have long recognized investor relations as a discipline. In this book, I use the term *owner relations* and interpret the function in a manner that is applicable to all types of organizations. Owner relations is a fundamental, indeed, the first job of a board. To help it fulfill this function, the board may employ others, including the CEO, but it is vital that the board recognizes that it always remains directly and fully accountable for the successful performance of owner relations.

The Importance of Owner Relations

Every board needs good relations with its owners because

- Owners' authority legitimizes the board's authority—or not!
- Owners are the people to whom the board ultimately has to account for everything.
- The interpretation and fulfillment of owners' best interests is what unifies board members in common cause; it is their group job.
- The board's interpretation of owners' best interests provides its ultimate touchstone for making difficult governing choices.

- The board's role as owners' representative distinguishes its role from the role of the organization's CEO and staff.

- A clear hold on the best interests of owners as a whole enables the board to insulate itself and the organization's CEO from pressures that could divert the organization from achieving its goals.

Designing Your Owner Relations Strategy

In the sections that follow, I outline the elements that a good owner relations strategy must address. Some of these elements will be explicitly stated in your Governance Process policies; others will simply inform your policies in this area.

Define Your Commitment to Owners   You will need to define your commitment to your owners and craft this definition into a clear statement that will ultimately become a part of your Governance Process policies. Even though we are not addressing how to write policies in this chapter, it will be useful to look at some examples of ownership statements in order to get a feel for the nature of the commitment to ownership that Policy Governance calls for. You will find some sample statements in Tool 3.1 at the end of this chapter.

Clarify Your Purpose   Your overall purposes in connecting with your owners are likely to fall into the following categories:

- To engage them in responsible ownership

- To be accountable to them

- To create the future they want

In the first category, place activities that have to do with educating owners about ownership and discussing what ownership means in the context of your organization and all the other roles being played within it. In the second category, include all the reporting you want to do about your organization's progress toward accomplishing your owner's wishes, including the annual report that you are obliged to give at your annual general meeting. In the last category, put whatever consultations you intend to hold with your owners to ensure that you are getting their input to help you develop your policies and particularly your Ends policies.

Create a Plan   Board time is very precious; there is so much to govern and so little time together to do the governing. Planning, therefore, will be a key to ensuring that your board follows through on its commitments, including the commitment to communicate with owners. A plan might set forth a time every year when the board will meet with owner representatives or when board representatives will meet with important groups within the ownership. It may identify a time when the board will send out questionnaires and gather information or, conversely, a time when the board will share important information with the ownership. (Tool 3.2 provides an example.) Your board's owner relations plan can use whatever time frame makes the most sense, but you will probably want to plan for a year at a time at the minimum and three years at maximum. Once your plan is complete, you can enter all the key dates on your annual board calendar. (An example of an annual board calendar can be found in Tool 8.8 at the end of Chapter Eight.)

Set the Context   If your board thinks that its owners are important, it is likely that your owners will be able to tell that from the way your board communicates with them. Indeed, however the board thinks about its owners is likely to show up in its communication. So it is very important for your board to discuss in advance the kind of relationship it wants with the owners of your organization and to let them know that before attempting to engage them in conversation. In other words, as in any relationship, you don't just jump in with assertions and demands; you establish or reestablish the relationship first.

Ask Intelligent Questions   As the adage goes, "Ask a stupid question, and you'll get a stupid answer." Conversely, treat people as intelligent human beings and face them with big, difficult questions, and they will rise to the occasion. In involving your owners in discussions about your organization's future, your board will often be asking them to think deeply about things that they have not considered before. For that you will need well-crafted questions, which, if you get them right, can produce a wealth of new perspectives and possibilities. It is important that your owners understand that there are no wrong answers and that you tell them how you are going to use their answers and then report back afterward about how you have used them. Do not promise more than you really mean to deliver.

As an illustration, let us take the board of a public hospital that wants input from its local community members as owners of the hospital on what they would like to see as the hospital's priorities in the future. Asking "What do you think this hospital should do in the future?" is likely to produce a long list of items that stem from people's own personal experience as users of the hospital. However, clearly showing those same people the sources and amounts of the hospital's likely income over the next thirty years and asking their opinions on the options that the board is considering for prioritizing particular results for particular patients within that income should produce some rich and meaningful owner input.

Be Truly Representative For the boards of organizations with large and diverse ownership, being representative cannot mean relying on the input of individual board members who have been elected or appointed by specific sections of the ownership. The whole board (and each of its members) is responsible for seeking to represent the interests of the entire ownership and has the resources to come up with far superior ways of finding out what ownership groups think, as illustrated below.

Choosing Your Tools for Communicating with Owners

Your board's every interaction with your owners, individually or in groups, is an opportunity to educate owners as well as to get their input. Many communication tools are available to help your board create more and better dialogue. In Table 3.1, you will find suggestions for various tools that your board might want to consider, depending on what it wants to achieve.

If your ownership is a large group, your board will need to consider whether to use tools that provide broad outreach, such as direct mail, mass media, or telephone polling. The Internet opens all sorts of possibilities, such as using other media to direct people to your Web site, which can offer information and interaction.

There are many useful book and Web-based resources on community engagement and social capital that your board might like to review in building its owner relations strategy. For example, *The Wisdom Of Crowds* by James Suroweicki (2004) provides fascinating perspectives on the value that can be derived from large scale outreach. Web sites on community engagement include a how-to guide from the Scottish Government (n.d.) and a collection of resources at www. bettertogether.org based on Robert Putnam and Lewis Feldstein's *Better Together: Restoring the American Community* (2003). Another example of a rich Web resource is the results of the *Proceedings* from the Fifth International Conference

Table 3.1
Board Tools for Owner Relations

	EDUCATING OWNERS	BEING ACCOUNTABLE TO OWNERS	CREATING THE FUTURE WITH OWNERS
Goals	Owners are informed about the privileges and responsibilities of ownership and the opportunities for exercising their legal and moral rights.	Owners are informed about the performance of their organization in relation to their wishes.	Owners' wishes are translated into informed decisions about organizational purpose and standards of ethics and prudence.
Promises	"We will always welcome and encourage your active participation as owners."	"We will regularly report to you in an open and honest manner."	"We will involve you in helping us to determine what our strategic outcomes and standards of ethics and prudence should be. We will take account of all your input and let you know how it influenced our decision making."
Tools to Consider	Owners' guide New board member search Brochure Web site Meetings Workshops Expert informants Newsletters Media releases Open board meetings	Annual meeting Annual report Videotaped board meetings Web site Newsletters Media releases Road shows	Advisory groups Roundtable discussions Joint meetings with other organizations Open forums Brown-bag lunch discussions Focus groups Needs assessments Impact studies

on Engaging Communities (2005), an initiative of the United Nations and the Queensland Government held in Brisbane, Australia, in 2005.

However, there is no need to get carried away. Even if your ownership is a large group, your board may be better off looking at more targeted options for reasons of cost and quality. For example, a focus group is often more productive than a public meeting. It is better to embark on a course that you are committed to fulfilling than to be overly ambitious and end up disappointing yourselves and your owners.

Tools for Responsible Ownership Engagement Thinking through what your board needs from your owners in order to govern responsibly on their behalf will help the board select the tools to use to promote responsible ownership engagement. Tool 3.3 at the end of this chapter is a summary of expectations that a board may have of its owners. This document is written to be shared with owners and can be adapted in any way that fits your organization.

As a general resource, why not create an owners' guide to your organization that board members can distribute to owners whenever and wherever they meet them? This tool can help board members, too, who can use it to remind themselves of the main points that they want to communicate to owners. Tool 3.4 at the end of this chapter provides a suggested table of contents for such a guide.

Tools for Being Accountable to Owners Every board's standard reporting tools are the annual report and financial accounts that are presented at the annual meeting of legal owners. These tools are good opportunities not only for reporting but also for more general owner education; thus, you might consider producing a short version of the annual report for wider distribution. Using the Policy Governance system, however, your board can go much further. As we shall see in the next two chapters, in the Policy Governance system, the policies that your board creates will be the standards that it uses for governing your organization on behalf of its owners. Thus, reporting to your owners becomes a straightforward matter of reporting on the criteria that have been established and how the organization is doing against them. Once your board has its policies in place, it may want to consider making them available to your owners. Many boards post their policies on their organization's Web site, along with an explanation of how they have organized themselves according to the Policy Governance system. Your board might also want to make its agendas and minutes available online.

In the same way that your CEO needs to be prepared to communicate with customers (however they may be referred to in your organization) in the event of a crisis, you as a board should also be prepared to account to your owners if there is a crisis. Being clear in advance about who is going to do what and how you are going to manage communications overall will help you act swiftly and appropriately if the need arises. During a crisis, the board needs to be honest and open and needs to take responsibility for any breakdown in the organization. Taking responsibility does not mean that the board has to jump into managing the organization. It does mean that the board needs to ensure that the CEO is clear about when the board expects the crisis to be resolved—and, therefore, compliance with relevant board policies restored—and the interim reporting the board requires along the way.

Tools for Evaluating Your Ownership Connection An essential part of the Policy Governance system is the board's evaluation of itself against all of its policy commitments, including its commitment to establishing and maintaining communication with its ownership. You will find more on the subject of board evaluation on pages 156–157 in Chapter Seven.

RELATIONS WITH OTHER STAKEHOLDERS

People need to communicate with your organization for all sorts of reasons, and however brilliant your owner education, your board members are bound to be approached for all sorts of reasons that are unrelated to its governance agenda. Your organization is, in effect, a web of different conversations, *all* of which the board needs to either conduct itself or ensure are properly governed.

Your board needs to converse with its owners, and your owners need to converse with the board. Your board needs to converse with your CEO, and your CEO needs to converse with your board. These are conversations for which the board cannot delegate its responsibility without breaking the owner-board-CEO chain of accountability. However, responsibility for the outcomes of other conversations necessary for the proper functioning of your organization, such as those with staff and customers, can and should be delegated to your CEO and governed through policies. as I shall discuss in the next three chapters. I say "can and should be delegated" because if the board retains direct responsibility for the outcomes of conversations with staff and customers, it inevitably takes its CEO off the hook for Ends fulfillment.

This principle does not mean that either the board as a whole or individual board members must give up directly engaging with staff or customers. In fact, conversation between the board and staff and between the board and customers becomes freer and more productive when everyone recognizes that the board's authority is only expressed in regularly monitored board policy, the fulfillment of which has been delegated to the CEO.

This picture is somewhat complicated by the need for conversations with regulators that are usually related to the CEO's domain but can be related to the board's domain—for example, when they impinge on bylaws or the development of board policy. The board can try to educate its regulators about how best to direct their communications or decide to direct all regulator communications to the board or the CEO according to whether they fall into the board or CEO domains of responsibility as set out in board policy.

MAKING OWNERSHIP COUNT

It is all very well to have a theory about the role of a board as representing the ownership within their organization, but the big question is how to put it into practice. As you will see in the rest of this book, Policy Governance is designed precisely to put this theory into practice. The implementation process starts when boards define their work in terms of their accountability to their owners and then define who their owners are. The second step is to develop succinct but all-encompassing written board policies that prescribe what should be produced for whom with what level of cost-efficiency and proscribe everything else. The third step is to delegate the fulfillment of those policies and then regularly and rigorously monitor their use in order to report back to owners, closing the circle of accountability.

Policy Governance makes ownership count because it treats the board's job as separable from all other jobs in the organization so that there can be clarity and accountability throughout the organization in fulfilling the wishes of its owners. The promise of Policy Governance, therefore, is enhanced organizational success for owners, and everything about Policy Governance flows directly from the ownership connection.

MOVING ON

This chapter has set the context for Policy Governance: the role of the board as owners' representative. Now it is time for the Policy Governance *system* itself to take the stage, starting with the design of the thing that lies at its core—a very special kind of policy.

TOOLS

TOOL 3.1 SAMPLE STATEMENTS OF A BOARD'S COMMITMENT TO ITS OWNERSHIP

Here are some typical statements that different types of boards make about their ownership. The last three examples illustrate how boards that are apparently very tightly constrained can create platforms for their leadership that will enable them to hold their owners to the standard of responsible ownership that they believe necessary for good governance. Clearly, their legal owners can overrule them any time they choose, but at least a broader ownership perspective gives the board somewhere to stand that gives them a meaningful role.

For a local government:

"The board will govern on behalf of the taxpayers of [*name of community*]."

For the self-appointed board of a social or political campaign:

"The board considers itself to be morally accountable to all those who are concerned with . . ."

For a government-appointed board:

"The board governs on behalf of [name of legal ownership body] in that body's capacity as representative of the public interest."

For a wholly owned subsidiary of a holding company:

"The board governs on behalf of [name of holding company] in that company's capacity as representative of the best interests of all its current and future shareholders."

For a company with a majority shareholder:

"The board considers itself accountable to all the shareholders of [name of company] as representatives of the best interests of all current and future owners."

 TOOL 3.2 SAMPLE OWNER RELATIONS PLAN

Sample Plan for November 2009–October 2010

OWNERSHIP LINKAGE ACTIVITY	MONTH	TARGET GROUP
Production of ownership guide for taxpayers	November	All owners
Annual specification of purposes for board liaisons with organizations that represent specific community groups	December	Selected community organizations as representatives of subsets of ownership
Distribution of board-designed ownership linkage questionnaire on Ends	February	Samples of all owner segments
Visits to key influencers by pairs of board members, along with a person who is not a board member serving as an observer and recorder	April	Key influencers
Web report to community on results of questionnaire and their impact on the board's decision making	June	All owners
Owners' meeting with facilitated discussion on performance report and Ends. Afterward, (1) Web report on the meeting and (2) thank-you letters to all meeting participants	August	All taxpayers and community organizations in one of the five geographical areas designated for owners' meetings. Other areas to be covered in subsequent years
Planning for year commencing November 2010	September	

Other Ownership Linkage Activities

Input from community speakers and attendance at community events according to board education plan for 2009–2010.

Implementation

Our Chief Governance Officer is the board member responsible for ensuring implementation of this plan. He or she may delegate authority to others to fulfill the plan but remains accountable for the plan. *Budget required:* The board needs to determine a budget for production of the ownership guide and questionnaire, questionnaire analysis, Web site work, travel costs, and summer owners' meeting costs, including facilitation.

TOOL 3.3 THE BOARD'S EXPECTATIONS OF THE OWNERS

This tool is designed for sharing with your owners to help them understand your role on their behalf and your expectations of them in their role as owners.

As the board of *[insert the name of your organization here]*, we are committed to governing your organization in a responsible manner. Here are some ways that you, our owners, can help us to do a good job on your behalf.

Care for the Whole Organization

We need our owners to care for our organization as a whole and to give us their input. If you have suggestions or concerns it will be extremely helpful if you can express them in relation to care of the organization as a whole.

Care for Yourself and Others

We need our owners to care for our organization on behalf of themselves *and* others and to give us their input. If you have suggestions or concerns, it will be extremely helpful if you can express them in relation to the best interests of all owners.

Engage as an Owner

Responsible owners engage with the organizations they own—for example, by attending annual owners' meetings, standing for board election, responding to board communications, or raising overall issues and concerns. We hope you will engage with us in helping to make your organization as successful as possible in fulfilling your wishes for it. Details of current opportunities for owners to engage with [*insert the name of your organization here*] are available at [*enter details*].

Keep the Owners' Communication Channel Open

Responsible owners do not block ownership communication channels with questions and issues that are about individual customer concerns. The board needs to approach its job from the perspective of ownership and therefore cannot allow itself to be dominated by individual customer concerns.

The board has ensured that staff members have a process for dealing with individual customer concerns that is easily accessible and treats customers in a timely, open, and respectful manner. Our policy is available at [*enter details*]. The board regularly monitors the organization's performance against this policy and handles any issues of noncompliance. If you have any complaints or concerns about the treatment of your own customer concerns or those of anyone you know, please contact [*enter appropriate staff contact information*].

TOOL 3.4 SUGGESTED TABLE OF CONTENTS FOR AN OWNER'S GUIDE

1. The importance of ownership

2. Your role as an owner

3. The role of the board as owner-representative

4. How you can participate in creating the board's leadership

5. The board and its operations

   a. Who we are, how we got here, what we do

   b. How we engage with and account to you as owners

   c. How we evaluate and report organizational performance

   d. How we evaluate and report board performance

6. Current and likely future ownership issues

7. Getting your issues/concerns to the right place

   a. The difference between owner and customer issues

   b. How, when and where you can input to the board as an owner

   c. How, when, and where you can provide input to staff as a customer

8. Our commitment to you and your organization

Understanding the *Policy* in Policy Governance

> *Instead of working towards intelligent accountability based on good governance, independent inspection, and careful reporting, we are galloping towards central planning by performance indicators, reinforced by obsessions with blame and compensation.*
>
> Onora O'Neill, "Onora O'Neill on Trust"

Jumping from talking about ownership straight into talking about policy may seem like a big leap. But if the board's role is to be the expression of ownership within your organization and you think of policy as the vehicle for that expression, it starts to make sense. Remember, the meaning of the word *policy* in the Policy Governance system is simply your board's values (or the things you care about on behalf of your owners, such as commitment to purpose and fiscal integrity) translated into written statements specifically designed to enable your board to be accountable for everything about your organization.

Moving from talking about ownership to talking about policy will make even more sense when you see how policies can be made into powerful control mechanisms for governing every aspect of your organization's current and future state. Once you have read this chapter, you should be in a position to understand

- What *policy* means in the Policy Governance system
- The overall Policy Governance system framework
- The different policy containers within the system and their purposes
- What the special policy architecture looks like

WHAT IS POLICY?

Policies in Policy Governance are written statements of values designed for the exercise of governing control. Because your board's job is to represent its owners, it follows that its work requires translating its owners' values into controls that enable it to govern and be accountable for everything your organization does and doesn't do. Given that your board is a small, part-time group, that's a pretty tall order when you think about how many things are going on every day in any given organization. People are arriving at work, leaving work, making decisions, not making decisions, meeting other people, organizing things, destroying things, creating things, buying things; the list is endless in even the smallest organization. And your board needs to control it all.

This chapter looks in detail at how your board members can best exercise meaningful control in accordance with their own values and the requirements of those whose authority legitimately supersedes their own.

TRADITIONAL WAYS THAT BOARDS EXERCISE CONTROL

The problem that boards face in exercising control over the organization that they hold in trust for their ownership is a very practical one. To illustrate the complexity of the problem, let's look at a mathematical equation. Take the number of hours your board meets every year and divide it into the number of hours your staff works.

If your board meets for three hours every month (which is highly optimistic, given that many boards meet quarterly at most), you have thirty-six hours of board time per year to govern your staff, who are probably working at least forty hours per week. Using even a fairly small organization with thirty staff members working forty-six weeks per year, we arrive at 55,200 hours, which means that the board has to use every hour of its time to govern 1,533 hours of everyone else's time. Whatever number you come up with, it will make the immensity of your board's control problem crystal clear.

Boards have tried to address the control problem in a number of ways. Before looking in detail at how board control is exercised through policies in the Policy Governance system, it may be helpful to briefly review traditional forms of control. Typically, these forms of control involve the use of three major tools: strategic plans (with their attendant performance indicators), budgets, and financial reports.

Strategic Plans or Business Plans

Unless you know where you want to go, it is impossible to get there; thus, boards have a strong interest in controlling their organization's future direction. The traditional way that boards go about controlling the future is by contributing to and approving management plans that contain performance indicators that can be tracked over time. This approach raises the following questions:

- How can the board ensure that the plans that staff prepare for board approval start from what should be achieved in the future rather than from what staff are engaged in today?

- How can the board act as an effective judge of plans and indicators that address the myriad of macro and micro internal issues that such plans and indicators typically address?

- Once the plan is approved by the board, are staff off the hook on whether it is the right plan?

- Once a strategy has been approved by the board, how can staff change it? As renowned academic and author on business and management Henry Mintzberg and his colleagues Bruce Ahlstrand and Joseph Lampel have pointed out, "Setting oneself on a predetermined course in unknown waters is a perfect way to sail straight into an iceberg" (Mintzberg, Ahlstrand, and Lampel, 2005). Indeed, *flexibility* has become a byword for good management as the speed of economic, social, and environmental change continues to increase. Organizational improvement expert Jim Clemmer (n.d.) speaks of the "faulty premise" of strategic planning—"that there is a right path, which can be determined in advance and then implemented." And according to Peter Drucker, whose career as a writer, consultant, and teacher spanned more than six decades, "The first change policy . . . has to be organized abandonment," in which "every product, every service, every process, every market, every distribution channel, every customer, and every end use" is regularly put "on trial for its life" (Drucker, 1999).

Whether or not strategic plans are good management tools, my point is that they are not governing tools because they are driven from the perspective of staff rather than of ownership. What matters to your owners is that your organization is producing the right benefit for the right people with the right cost-efficiency; in other words, what matters to owners is what the organization is *for*—the destination rather than the journey.

Budgets

- Typically, strategic plans give rise to budgets; thus, budgets therefore raise all the same issues as strategic plans when it comes to control. On the plus side, budgets show boards the likely costs of groups of items and of some individual items on which staff intend to spend money in the coming year. Reviewing such figures therefore gives boards the opportunity to question whether their staff is intending to spend money on the right things at the right cost. Over the year, reviewing budget figures also gives boards the opportunity to track whether staff estimates were correct, and if they were not correct, why not. Control through budget reviews, however, raises the following questions:

- Can board members truly be expected to understand all that lies behind the numbers they are approving?

- What will happen when the approximate numbers approved by the board change, as they inevitably will?

- What are the numbers designed to achieve?

- What is the board's role in deciding what the numbers are designed to achieve?

Trying to control an organization through budget approval is asking both too much and too little of the board. It doesn't provide a way for the board to chart an overall course for the organization, and at the same time, it asks that the board have a grasp of organizational detail that is simply not possible.

Financial Reports

Financial reports are about the past. A review of the past may help your board to consider what it needs to control about the future but does not, in itself, control the future. Indeed, knowing how something went in the past is a very unreliable predictor of the future; this is the problem with trying to govern by monitoring budget variances. The story of my typical annual Christmas gift shopping day illustrates the point. As I set off, I have a financial plan. I have a number of people to buy gifts for and an overall budget. As a guide, I also have in mind roughly how much I am going to spend to get what I want for each person. Notice that if you were to accost me at noon that day, you would probably find lots of variances on my budget due to a combination of unpredictable occurrences such as these:

- I found the perfect gift for someone for much less than I anticipated.
- Something I thought of as a "must have" turned out to be far more expensive than I anticipated.
- I became overwhelmed by desire for a large hot chocolate after a major session in the bookshop.

Yet you would be totally wrong to assume that this means that I will have failed at the end of the day. I will still achieve my target by making the necessary adjustments as I go. Neither tracking variances from a budget based on a plan that inevitably must vary nor receiving information about your actual financial condition after anyone can do anything about it represent the kind of proactive, comprehensive, and coherent owner control that boards need to exert.

Boards that use such traditional control methods are usually well aware of the challenging nature of their job. They know that turning up at meetings ready to ask questions about documents prepared by staff can provide insights into some things but not the comprehensive control and assurance that seems to be expected of them by their regulators and stakeholders. Thus, boards using traditional control methods have a tendency to veer between too much control and too little control. Boards with CEOs whom they trust tend to operate in a fairly relaxed mode, believing that because their CEO is likely to know best, it makes the best sense to let him or her get on with things. However, boards that are uncertain about their CEO or whose organizations experience problems move quickly toward taking a lot of direct control into their own hands. The problem is that moving back and forth between very little control and a lot of control does not provide the consistency needed for proactive, comprehensive, and coherent owner control.

A NEW WAY FOR BOARDS TO EXERCISE CONTROL

This book is about a new way for boards to exercise control. Policy Governance differs from traditional ways because it offers boards a complete system through which they can exercise comprehensive, consistent, proactive, and coherent owner control.

Control That Starts from the Top

Policy Governance control starts from the top. In other words, Policy Governance starts from the perspective of those from whom the board gets its authority to operate—the ownership. As was explained in Chapter Three, a successful board and hence a successful organization is one that fulfills its owners' purpose. Although organizations with passive boards can be successful on their own terms, without the board's active leadership, there is no guarantee that that success will accord with owners' definitions of success. And if your organization's success is not success in owners' terms, it cannot legitimately be called *success*. For example, a theater company might have a string of sold-out musicals, but if the owners created the company to showcase cutting-edge drama, the organization cannot rightfully claim that it is successful. A grocery chain may make a large annual profit, but if owners' interests lie in sacrificing immediate profit to ensure continuing competitiveness, success is a moot point.

Using Policy Governance enables boards to provide leadership in the form of a framework of clearly written policies within which all the different parts of an organization can be aligned in pursuit of a clearly defined vision of success. To provide a framework, you cannot, by definition, jump into the middle of any issue; you have to stand back and take a broader, longer-term perspective. Thus, boards must stand slightly outside the organization in order to see the whole and how best to control it. The ownership perspective gives boards the highest possible perspective within the organization, a perspective from which a policy framework can be created that encompasses the work of the whole organization, including the work of the board itself.

Control Through Policy Containers

Policy Governance exercises control by expressing board values as written policies that are organized into specially designed categories or containers. Policy Governance does not, however, assume that any board's values are the same as any other board's.

Every set of owners has its own values. Every board is surrounded by advice and regulation. Every organization has its own history and circumstances. Every board needs to take account of all these things in formulating its own values. Policy Governance is not about the content of such values but rather about organizing them into a set of effective long-term controls. For emphasis, let me repeat the same thought another way: Policy Governance is not about telling your board what values it should have but rather about how best to organize its values so that they can be most effective.

Organizing your life requires categorizing and sorting things into like piles in a like manner so that they can be used efficiently. Wardrobes are overall containers for our clothing within which we have separate smaller containers (such as shelves and rods) for different items. Calendars are overall containers for our activities in which we have separate smaller containers for each day's activities. Computers are overall containers for our documents in which we have separate smaller containers (or folders) for each sort of document. Organization through the use of containers makes it possible for us to more readily control our lives because we can

- See what we have and what we don't have

- Find what we want when we need it

- Maintain what we have to the standard we want

Similarly, Policy Governance is an overall container for the expression of your board's policies within which there are separate containers and subcontainers for each category of board concern. I will introduce the categories of concern covered by each of these containers and subcontainers here, before going into far more detail on them. All categories of board concern in Policy Governance are first divided between two containers: ends (which encompass the board's

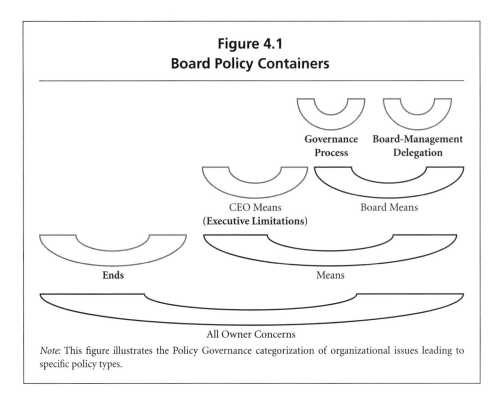

Figure 4.1
Board Policy Containers

Governance Process

Board-Management Delegation

CEO Means
(Executive Limitations)

Board Means

Ends

Means

All Owner Concerns

Note: This figure illustrates the Policy Governance categorization of organizational issues leading to specific policy types.

concerns about the benefits that the organization needs to produce, for whom, and at what cost) and means (which encompass the board's concerns about everything else). These two broad containers together are then subdivided into ends, governance process, board-management delegation, and executive limitations. Figure 4.1 shows how the policy containers fit together. You may find it useful to refer to this figure as you read through the following discussion of which policies belong in each container and why.

THE FIRST TWO CONTAINERS: ENDS AND MEANS

Before any further classification is done, the Policy Governance system requires that all board issues be separated into issues of what the organization is for and issues of how the organization goes about what it is for (such as staff compensation and board meeting conduct). This separation is reflected in the labels typically attached to the first two containers within the Policy Governance system: *ends* and *means.*

The Ends Control Container

Getting organized starts with sorting everything you have into containers of like items. As I just stated, the first and most important separation you need to make as a board is between the following two categories:

- Issues of what your organization is for
- Issues of how your organization should conduct itself while accomplishing what it is for

The effectiveness of Policy Governance control depends on this separation being done properly, for mixing issues of purpose with other issues will confound your purpose.

We are surrounded by examples of confusion between issues of purpose and other issues—and the sad results. For example, most hospitals would probably say that they exist for the purpose of helping patients achieve the best possible health and well-being (or some variant thereof). Yet many public hospitals exist in environments that insist on compliance with targets pertaining to how they should go about their work, which can overtake their focus on purpose. Being able to admit and discharge patients quickly may be a good measure of the efficiency of a hospital's procedures, but hospitals do not exist to have efficient procedures. As many patients know, to their detriment, unless efficient procedures are judged in their proper context—that is, by whether they contribute to the achievement of the best possible health outcomes, they can be life-threatening.

Having created a container for issues concerned with your organization's purpose, you will need to label it. You can call it *Ends* (which is the term used in Policy Governance and the term I will use in this book) or *Strategic Outcomes* or whatever suits your board. Whatever you call it, for the Policy Governance system to work properly, it is vital that you keep the content in this container strictly to your definition of why your organization exists in terms of *whose lives you are trying to affect, with what result, and with what cost-efficiency.* In other words, *Ends* in the Policy Governance system are not typical expressions of mission or goals but the board's answers to three very specific questions. The design and content of the Ends container are described in much more detail in the next chapter.

The Means Control Container

The next section focuses on the design of the containers for all your non-Ends concerns, which in the Policy Governance system, as stated earlier, fall under the heading of *means* (which is the term I will use in this book). In the Policy Governance system, organizations and all their inner workings and activities—including the workings and activities of boards themselves—fall into the means container.

SUBDIVIDING THE MEANS CONTAINER BETWEEN BOARD AND CEO MEANS

Because it contains all the board's values about matters that are not to do with what the organization is for, the means container includes items that are pertinent only to the operation of the board and items that are pertinent only to the operation of the organization under the CEO. Therefore, for the sake of clear classification, the Policy Governance system requires that the means container be further subdivided into one for controlling CEO means issues and one for controlling board means issues.

The Container for Controlling the CEO's Means

In Policy Governance, the container for all board values that govern CEO means is typically labeled *Executive Limitations* or *Management Limitations,* but it could equally as well be headed *Risk Management Framework* or anything else that denotes that these values describe the boundary between acceptable and unacceptable CEO means. In this book, I call this container or category *Executive Limitations.*

The Container for Controlling Board Means

The board means container contains all policies about the operation of your board: your board's code of conduct, how meetings will be run, the role of the board chair or CGO, how the board will find and orient new board members, and so forth. Board means policies are also where you specify to whom you are delegating your authority for the management of the organization and how you will monitor, evaluate, and reward proper use of that authority. John and Miriam Carver's writings suggest that for clarity and convenience, the container for board means should be further subdivided into the two areas that I just described. The first container is for policies about the organization of the board's job and thus is named *Governance Process.* The second container is for policies about how the board connects its authority to its organization's executive and is named *Board-Management Delegation.*

So now I have described four containers that can be used to encompass all owner concerns. They can be labeled however you want as long as you are meticulous about the separation between Ends and means and between the board's means and the CEO's means, but in the Policy Governance system, they are typically labeled as in Figure 4.1.

DESIGNING POLICIES WITHIN THE POLICY CONTAINERS

Now that you have identified four containers within which your board can organize all of its values, the board needs to fill those containers not just any old way but, rather, with carefully designed policies. In Policy Governance, this work is at the heart of your board's job, and it is essential that your board undertake it carefully. Just consider the power that your board has in addition to its accountability. In principle, no one in your organization has the right to ignore what your board says. If anyone wants to contradict your board, their only appeal is to the legal ownership, and your organization's legal ownership may be very difficult to reach or may consist entirely of board members anyway. Using power wisely is, therefore, an essential governance obligation.

Policies are key to fulfilling the obligation to use power wisely, for what tools other than words does any board have for expressing its power? Hence, wise use of board power means wise use of words, which means that your board needs to be very aware of its purpose and the impact of its words on others. In the remainder of this chapter, I first examine the pitfalls of traditional approaches to designing policies and then I describe what it takes to design strong policies. Finally, I discuss how to maintain your policies.

Pitfalls of Traditional Policy Design

Policies need to be designed such that they can be actively managed. Said another way, if a board has policies that are so numerous or haphazardly constructed that it cannot know what the policies say or don't say, nor identify contradictions between them, nor improve on them over time, nor monitor whether they are having the desired impact, then they have more empty rhetoric than governing policy.

Words do not have to be numerous to be very powerful; quite the reverse, in fact. The persistence of an urban legend evidences our appreciation of the point: the legend holds that the Ten Commandments are 179 words long and Archimedes's principle is 67 words long, whereas U.S. government regulations on the sale of cabbage are 26,911 words long (Mikkelson, 2007)!

A major issue with traditional board policies is that they tend to accumulate in response to events and issues as they arise. Policies, therefore, are often scattered across the board's minutes in the form of recorded decisions made in particular meetings, which makes them hard to find when needed. In addition, policies are likely to be haphazard in terms of what they do and do not control and may even be contradictory.

Things don't get much better even when boards make a concerted effort to create one list of standing instructions or statements of delegated authority for their staff. The policies contained in such lists and statements always fall far short of proactive, comprehensive, and coherent owner control, for much the same reasons I have just detailed. First, the policies cover only some aspects of the organization's operations (for example, expenditure limits or hiring of staff). Second, the policies generally consist of a long list of items for which the CEO is required to get the board's approval, thereby making it clear that instead of providing a systematic governance framework within which staff are free to operate, the board is going to make most decisions itself without any pre-stated criteria. In fact, lack of good policy design leaves boards with no choice but to stick with approving many items of business, which is the source of many governance ills, including the following.

Ineffective Use of Time   Approval without pre-stated policy criteria can lead to ineffective use of both staff and board time. For staff, having a board that must approve individual propositions typically means spending time trying to guess what the board would like to see. So there is a policy design issue of whether staff time would be better used if staff could start from knowing what the board would like to see. For boards, giving approvals typically means spending time trying to guess what should be probed further and what can be left alone. So there is a policy design issue of whether board time would be better used if boards could start from knowing what would make any proposition approvable so that they could focus their probing on just those things.

Muddled Accountability   Approval without pre-stated policy criteria can also create confusion about accountability for outcomes. Once a board approves something, it presumably puts itself directly on the hook for the outcome of that decision, which presumably exonerates whoever requested the approval from future responsibility for how that decision turns out. In my experience, the reality in such cases is that who is accountable usually remains uncertain. In other words, in such cases, no one is accountable.

Haphazard Control   Without explicit and agreed-on policy criteria for judging whether things are "approvable," decision making is inevitably a pretty random process not only in terms of what does and does not get approved but also in terms of what gets on the agenda. And trying to differentiate between board and staff agendas on the basis of vague terms such as *major, substantial, strategic,* and *sizable* in contrast to terms like *micromanagement, procedural, detailed,* and *wordsmithing* doesn't help. What is a minor detail to one board member may be a significant issue to another, resulting in an impasse that is impossible to resolve unless the board has some criteria for judging which is which.

Powerful Policy Design

As I discussed earlier, in Policy Governance, policies are values specifically designed for the purpose of exercising *governing* control, which means that they are designed not to make decisions for people but to create a framework of values within which people can be allowed to make their own decisions. Going a bit further, we could say that the *policy* in Policy Governance is *a comprehensive body of standing controls through which the board governs all present and future decisions.* To form a body of standing controls suitable for governing, the board must ensure that its values are

- In written form and so always available to all those who need to operate from them
- Justifiable in terms of owners' best interests
- At a high enough level to provide long-term direction
- Sufficient to form a comprehensive framework of standards within which people can get on with what they need to do
- Applicable to as many similar issues as possible

- Integrated so that they form a coherent whole

- Organized to enable relevant values to be found, used, and improved

- Separated into Ends and means

- Concise enough to be managed and monitored at a reasonable cost

- Clear enough to be understood by all those who need to operate from them

And to provide real control, the board must ensure that its values remain true to the criteria on the preceding list, no matter who sits on the board today or tomorrow, no matter who the CEO may be, and no matter how the organization's circumstances may change. Constantly changing policies may not cost a board a lot of time and effort, but inside their organization, they cause chaos and consequent loss of time, money, and momentum. A report from the United Nations emphasizes the need for responsible use of the power of words in the public sector: "Nothing saps the public trust more quickly than the confusion resulting from inapplicable, vague, conflicting and forever changing legal provisions, which compound the costs of business, discourage enterprise or, worse still, afford knaves and villains windows of opportunity at public expense. Labyrinthine provisions and legislative loopholes both serve to exacerbate the practice of rewarding the least deserving, and of defrauding the public, thus slowly but surely, creating a climate of collective alienation, cynicism and greed" (United Nations, 2001, p. 76).

Policy Governance offers powerful policy control that meets all the criteria on the preceding list with the help of two important elements—the use of policy ranges and the delegation of authority to act within any reasonable interpretation of those ranges.

Control Through Policy Ranges Depending on how individual policies are designed within each container, they can govern either a very large number of actions and further decisions or very few. For example, let's say that in your family, courtesy is highly valued. And let's say that this value is often strained by the behavior of little Peter, who has particular difficulty with being courteous to Aunt Jean when he sees her every year on her birthday. Well, you could create a policy that explicitly states that Peter should be courteous to Aunt Jean on her birthday, and then as problems arise with other individuals, you could create other policies that would address those problems. These clearly would be policies that cover a very narrow range, and it might be necessary to develop quite a few of them over time to cover all the possible ways that family members can fail to be courteous. Alternatively, you could simply create a single policy that covers a broader range of behavior by stating that everyone must always be courteous to everyone else. You might want to further define this policy with a few narrower policies (see the sample policies in the next section), or you may find that this broad policy is all you need.

Whatever you decide, it is important that you create the minimum number of policies you feel is necessary to serve and protect your owners. The more you rely on creating many narrow policies, the more they become impossible to use as governing controls because it becomes harder and harder to manage and monitor them. The challenge in managing and monitoring board policy created using traditional policy design can be truly immense. According to Paul Bullen of Management Alternatives Pty Ltd in Coogee, Australia, for a small organization with less than ten staff members, a policy manual of up to eighty pages "could include most of the significant policies the organization may need," whereas a large organization might need a series of "organizational manuals" that could include a corporate plan, a strategic plan, a services plan, service policies and procedures, human resource policies and procedures, and administration policies and procedures, "the last four of which could run to hundreds (or even thousands) of pages each" (Bullen, n.d.).

The Policy Governance system addresses the need to keep the number of board policies down to a manageable and monitorable number.

Sequencing Policy Ranges   The Policy Governance system requires that policies within each of the four containers be carefully sequenced according to their ranges of control, from broadest to narrowest. Here is the process:
In each of the four containers,

1. Create a one-sentence policy that controls the entire range of possible owner concerns in that container. In Policy Governance, we often refer to this all-encompassing policy as a *global statement.*

2. Consider what further containers you need to create to control your next most specific level of concerns.

3. Create a one-sentence policy that controls the entire range of possible owner concerns in each of those containers.

4. Repeat steps 2 and 3 until your board feels that it can responsibly accept any reasonable interpretation of what it has said.

Once your board has completed this process, it will find that it has achieved something quite remarkable: it has controlled all possible owner concerns in far, far fewer words than anyone might have believed possible. To illustrate this economy, let's use the policy sequencing process for the family mentioned in the preceding section, and let's say that they create a policy container called *Family Courtesy.*

1. They create their broadest policy within the Family Courtesy container: "Everyone must always be courteous to all relatives."

2. They create a container at the next level called *Family Birthdays* (perhaps along with other containers at the same level, such as Family Visiting).

3. They create their broadest policy within the Family Birthdays container: "Family members will acknowledge all relatives' birthdays."

4. They decide that they can stop at this level in the Family Birthdays container, for they see that they no longer need a policy about little Peter and his aunt's birthday nor, indeed, about any one family birthday, for they have covered all eventualities for everyone with one brief policy that they are willing to accept any reasonable interpretation of.

To summarize, when a board uses the policy sequencing component of the Policy Governance system, there are far, far fewer policies than possible actions, and decisions that will be taken in the light of those policies.

Stopping at the Point at Which Any Reasonable Interpretation Will Do   Ensuring that your board stops creating policies at the level at which it feels that it can responsibly accept any reasonable interpretation of what it has said is vital if your board is to delegate anything. In other words, unless the only value that your owners are going to realize from your organization is what your board members are able to personally produce, it will have to give its delegate or delegates some room for discretion.

Yes, your board is accountable for everything, but in order to delegate, board members must be able to fulfill that accountability by holding others to account rather than by doing things themselves. And the board's delegates must have some freedom, for clearly you can't hold anyone to account for the results of decisions and actions over which you gave them no choice. If I tell you exactly how to do something and you follow my instructions but it doesn't turn out as I had hoped, it is surely me, not you, who is accountable for the outcome.

In any case, most people would agree that freedom is an essential ingredient for success in today's world and that the command-and-control paradigm is on its last legs. Today, success involves creating the conditions for people to be self-motivated and for organizations to be innovative and flexible enough to respond to ever more rapidly changing opportunities and threats. For the board's delegates to have real freedom within board policy—the freedom to innovate and flex as they see necessary to achieve the board's Ends—they must be given the authority to make any reasonable interpretation of that policy.

Because the aforementioned family constrained itself from going to a further level of specificity, little Peter can acknowledge his aunt's birthday in any way he chooses. For example, he could wish her a happy birthday in person or on the phone, or he could make her a card, or he could add his name to a card that his mother is sending, or he could make a cake, buy a present, and throw a big party. The family has given up the right to dictate the form of Peter's acknowledgment and the right to complain about Peter's choice on any other grounds than reasonableness. If they wanted cards sent, they could have said so, but they didn't; they left the choice up to any reasonable interpretation by each family member.

In fact, the world would come to a grinding halt without the concept of "any reasonable interpretation." Ultimately, things won't work unless we can deal with being accountable while someone else does the work. Airlines have to let their pilots fly their planes. Hospitals have to allow their surgeons sufficient freedom to perform operations. School teachers have to be allowed to teach. Why shouldn't boards allow their CGOs and CEOs to do their jobs, too?

By ceasing to define narrower policy ranges at the point at which it can accept any reasonable interpretation of what it has said, your board will be creating the free space that will allow its delegates to use all their creativity, talent, experience, and commitment to make happen what the board wants to happen. Your board will also have answered one of the most challenging questions that every board faces—"Who does what?"—and answered it with enormous precision. For once your policies are in place, it will be clear that any decision or action that can be justified as falling within any reasonable interpretation of your policies is your delegates' domain, and anything that doesn't is yours. This concept allows a board to have the clarity about its role that so many governance pundits call for but have no idea how to achieve.

Monitoring "Any Reasonable Interpretation"   Allowing your delegates the freedom to make any reasonable interpretation of your policies does not meant that they can abdicate responsibility for their use of that freedom—far from it. As you will see in Chapter Seven, you will be regularly and rigorously monitoring every policy you create in order to ensure that it is indeed being reasonably interpreted and acted on. And your board will be the ultimate judge of the reasonability of all your delegates' interpretations.

The process starts straight away. As soon as your board has established its policies, its delegates (your CEO in regard to Ends and Executive Limitations policies and your CGO in regard to your Governance Process and Board-Management Delegation policies) need to get going on producing their interpretations so that they can act in accordance with the policies and begin collecting data for the relevant monitoring reports, many of which will be due within the year—and some within three months—a process that we will discuss in depth in Chapter Seven.

MAINTAINING YOUR POLICIES

Once established, your policy framework should be in constant use by your board and its delegates, and all your board's work should be cumulative, recorded, and easily referenced. In Policy Governance, policies are dynamic because as regularly monitored written definitions of what is required, they are constantly referred to and reviewed. Your CEO and staff will be consulting your policies as issues arise in order to establish whether their current topic of concern is a matter for any reasonable interpretation by the CEO or whether it is a board issue. Your board members, too, should find themselves referring frequently to their Ends and Executive Limitations policies in order to establish what they have already said to their CEO and assess its adequacy. Perhaps even more frequently, your board members will find themselves referring to the policies that guide your board operations—your Governance Process and Board-Management Delegation policies. In fact, every item at every board meeting should be explicitly linked to one or more of your policies so that you can see exactly where the item is situated in your governance control framework.

Thus, if you are truly using the Policy Governance system, your policies will not sit on the shelf and gather dust. In fact, if you are truly using the Policy Governance system, your policies should become an increasingly accurate and succinct repository of all your values as they evolve over time. Certainly, you want to keep your direction as consistent as possible, for, as I discussed on page 82 there is a big price to pay for board inconsistency; however, what you want to say today in your policies is not necessarily what you will want to say tomorrow. The world does not stand still, and whether or not the use of your policies throws up suggestions for change, it is a very good idea to institute a regular review of your policies to see whether they require updating.

MOVING ON

Now, however, the time has come for your board to start filling in your policy containers. In the next chapter, we will begin with the Ends policies. Figure 4.2 offers a visual representation of how policies in the four main policy areas relate to one another. Note that numbering systems and policy titles can vary from board to board and particularly when it comes to Ends. Figure 4.2 illustrates a numbering system that combines letters and numbers, whereas Tables 6.1, 6.2, and 6.3 in Chapter Six use a number-only system. The two left-hand quadrants govern the work of the board and the two right-hand quadrants the work of the CEO. The unoccupied space at the center is the room left for any reasonable interpretation by the CGO (on the left-hand side) and by the CEO (on the right-hand side). The important things to remember are to fill each of the four containers with only those policies that are appropriate to that container and to carefully craft these policies in sequence, moving from the broadest to the narrowest range of your concerns. That process is covered in the next two chapters.

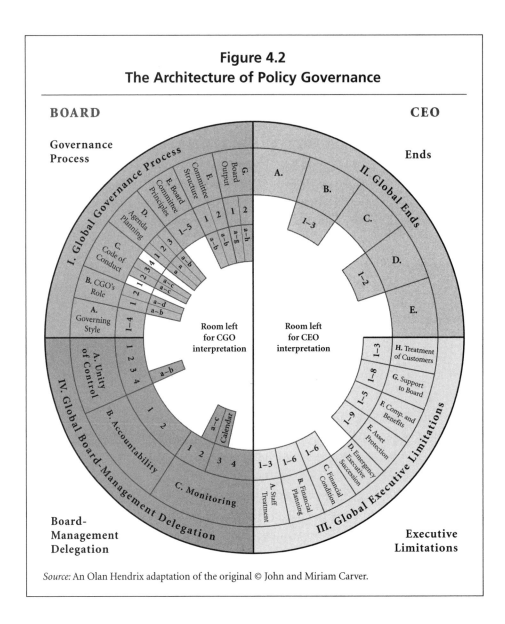

Figure 4.2
The Architecture of Policy Governance

BOARD

Governance
Process

CEO

Ends

Room left
for CGO
interpretation

Room left
for CEO
interpretation

Board-
Management
Delegation

Executive
Limitations

Source: An Olan Hendrix adaptation of the original © John and Miriam Carver.

What Does Your Ownership Want?

Creating Ends Policies

Perfection of means and confusion of goals seem—in my opinion—to characterize our age.

Albert Einstein

This chapter is going to help you understand how to create policies that outline the ends you want your organization to achieve.

Creating Ends policies is hard work, but it is some of the most valuable work your board will ever do, for it goes to the heart of what your organization exists for. People create organizations to create the future they want. If boards do not take the lead, the future will happen anyway, but it will happen by staff design or by sheer chance rather than at owners' behest. And if the future that gets created isn't the future that owners want, how can it be said to be the right future for your organization?

The Policy Governance system enables boards to lead their organizations into the future by defining "true north" through policies that are situated in the policy container that is usually called *Ends* but could be called *Strategic Outcomes* or *Results* or *Goals* or *Success* or whatever your board prefers, as long as the container maintains the distinctness of Ends as set out in this chapter.

Before you know how to ride a bike, most of your energy is focused on finding and maintaining your balance. However, the moment you know how to ride your bike, your focus shifts away from the mechanics of traveling and toward where you want to go. For Policy Governance boards, Ends policies are the most challenging and the most rewarding to create but also a large part of the reason for adopting Policy Governance, for they are all about where you want to go. In other words, once you have become familiar with operating through the Policy Governance system and therefore have all the controls in place for making sure your organization is operating safely, you will find that you have the time to focus on what matters most—what it's all for.

Your controls for making sure your organization is operating safely are the policies that govern the means employed by your CEO and board, which are detailed in the next chapter. In fact, boards often create those safety policies before looking at Ends policies (see page 177 in Chapter Eight), but in this book, we are going to tackle Ends policies first because they flow so directly from the discussion of ownership in Chapter Three. While owners' concerns about safety tend to be very similar, what owners are trying to accomplish can vary much more widely; therefore, owners' wishes are most sharply differentiated in Ends policies.

Once you have read this chapter, you will understand

- What Ends are
- How Ends flow from ownership
- The difference between Ends and means
- How to establish your organization's Ends policies

DEFINING YOUR DESTINATION

Having clarified who your ownership is, your board is ready to determine its Ends policies. Ends could also be described as your organization's destination, its bottom line, the difference your organization exists to make in the world, or what your organization is for. And, second only to your definition of ownership, there are no more important policies than these, for their accomplishment provides the rationale for everything else you do.

The special design of Ends policies in the Policy Governance system makes them extremely powerful tools for directing your organization. Using that design, a change of just one or two words in describing your destination will cause everything in your organization to turn on its in axis in order to go where the board says. If power is the ability to change a lot with a little, you can't get much more powerful than that. Mission statements and vision statements, of course, are intended to do the same thing—to state what an organization is for—but unless they use the design of Ends policies, they are not the same thing at all.

Mission statements and vision statements certainly express a board's aspirations, but they lack the specific crafting of Ends that transforms aspirations into precision tools for holding delegates accountable for their performance.

All boards use words, but on Policy Governance boards, words are the board's power over their organization and are used very carefully and specifically to create and deliver that power.

How Ends Provide Clear Direction

Ends policies are not fond hopes but precision tools for governing. As such, they provide

- Clear direction—"true north"
- Efficiency—the unification, integration, and alignment of everything an organization is and does
- The criteria for assessing both easy and difficult means choices
- Benchmarks for success or progress

Charging your CEO with the fulfillment of Ends and then holding him or her accountable gives your board an immensely powerful lever that will automatically lead to the most effective means choices. Also, when your Ends policies are fully developed, your board will have defined the ultimate yardstick for measuring your organization's success. To develop its Ends policies, your board will need to interpret your owners' desires for the future in regard to three questions:

1. What difference do we want to make?
2. For which people?
3. With what level of cost-efficiency?

Answering the Ends Questions

For your organization, the answers to some of the Ends questions may be clear, but in answering them, most boards find themselves facing critical choices that have hitherto been made only by default—in other words, without conscious deliberation or agreement. The following discussion of each question should help your board's deliberations.

Ends Question 1: What Difference Do You Want to Make? Board members typically give their time and energy because they want to make a difference, and people are typically attracted to your organization because of the difference you make. Notice that the first part of an Ends policy—the difference you want to make—is a difference outside the organization, a difference in people's lives.

If your board members find themselves talking about a difference within your organization, they are not talking about Ends. Services, programs, initiatives, technologies, and buildings are not Ends; they are things that your organization may use to produce its Ends, but they are not what your organization is for. Your organization might exist to enable certain people to acquire accommodations, health, wealth, peace, knowledge, or many other things, but it certainly does not exist to perpetuate itself. Organizations can be very, very busy to no great effect. That's why Ends policies do not include effort words nor describe activities; they give no points for trying.

For example, Ends policies do not describe organizational purpose in terms such as "XYZ Organization exists to create . . ." or "to provide . . ." or "to develop . . ." this or that or the other thing. Instead, Ends policies speak to which people's lives will be different and what that difference will be if owners' definition of success has been achieved, because, of course, no one can know what needs to be created or provided or developed until this definition has been made. Thus, as you can see in the examples at the end of this chapter (Tools 5.1–5.6), the language of Ends is much more like "XYZ Organization exists so that [*name of beneficiaries*] have [*description of outcome in beneficiaries' lives*] at a justifiable level of cost-efficiency."

Ends Question 2: Whom Do You Want to Affect? Your board may be very clear about who it wishes to benefit from your organization's existence, but for many boards, this is not an entirely straightforward question. For example, an orchestra might be a publicly owned body seeking to affect its local community, or it might be a body that is owned by local music lovers that seeks to affect other actual and potential music lovers, or it might be a workers' cooperative that seeks to benefit its musician members.

Other organizations may call people *members,* implying that they are both owners and beneficiaries when the actuality may be more complex. Take, for example, the organizations that exist purely for the self-regulation of professionals such as doctors, lawyers, and nurses. While the professionals may be called *members,* and think of themselves as beneficiaries, they are in fact obliged to operate for the benefit of the public on whose behalf the government has given the profession the right to self-regulate.

Other issues that may arise as your board considers whom it wants to affect involve the treatment of those who could benefit from your organization's work but who are not its target beneficiaries. Should they be served at all? Should they be served only on a full cost-recovery or profit basis? In either case, if serving them is not part of what your organization is for, anything your board might want to say about them is by definition a matter of Executive Limitations rather than Ends.

If your organization is a for-profit corporation, the people whose lives you primarily wish to affect are your shareholders. Of course, your ability to benefit your shareholders will depend to a very large degree on your staff's ability to offer value to customers. When car manufacturers envision every household having one of their cars or financial services advisors think about how they can increase their clients' financial security, they are certainly thinking about benefits to customers, but their ultimate purpose is to provide benefits to shareholders.

You could say that the owners in both nonprofit and for-profit organizations are very similar in that they are seeking personal satisfaction from obtaining benefits for other people. But there is a significant difference. For owners of nonprofits, the fact that satisfaction does not include financial reward to themselves as owners is not a problem. For owners of for-profit organizations, lack of financial rewards for themselves as owners would ultimately lead to the cessation of their business. Thus, in nonprofits, issues pertaining to benefits to customers (or clients or whatever they are called) are normally Ends issues, whereas in for-profits, issues of customer benefits are normally means issues. In other words, for nonprofit boards, their organization's choices about who should be customers and what benefits they should get are part of defining their ultimate purpose. On the other hand, for the boards of for-profit organizations, their organization's choices about who should be their customers and what benefits those customers should get are normally just steps along the way to helping their organization fulfill its ultimate purpose of benefiting its shareholders.

Ends Question 3: What Level of Cost-Efficiency Do You Want to Achieve? The third and final element of an Ends policy ensures that your organization represents the value-for-money that your board feels obliged to require. This question is neither about your organization's financial status nor about fundraising, for by holding your CEO rigorously to account for achieving your Ends within Executive Limitations, your board will automatically be requiring your CEO to secure the maximum possible funds (with or without the board's help; see more on this topic on page 167 in Chapter Eight) to achieve the maximum possible results while avoiding financial jeopardy.

This Ends question is about the efficiency with which your organization produces its Ends within the limits of whatever funds it may have at any time. In other words, what is the standard that your board believes should be used to justify the value of your organization's results as worth the amount of resources that were devoted to producing them?

The board's definition of the level of cost-efficiency that it seeks as purchasing agent on behalf of owners must always be present at least at the broadest, highest level of Ends policy. For example, the Ends policy of a cancer care charity might be something like "XYZ exists so that people living with cancer have the information and support necessary to secure the best possible care in a manner that justifies the resources expended." In the Ends policy of a private corporation, you might find language such as "Our company exists in order to provide us with a return on our investment of financial, human, and relational capital that we will see as having made that investment worthwhile."

Other typical Ends language on cost-efficiency includes

- "At a level that justifies the funds invested"
- "At a justifiable level of cost-efficiency"
- "With a level of cost-efficiency exceeding that typically achieved by other similar organizations"
- "In a manner that represents good value for money"
- "In a manner that results in an excellent overall cost-benefit ratio"
- "To the extent that justifies the resources expended"

Having defined cost-efficiency at the level of your broadest Ends policy, your board may wish to further define it at the next most specific levels, or it may wish to stop at that and leave further definition to your CEO's interpretation. Deciding worth at the next most specific levels of Ends typically comes down to addressing the relative priority of different outcomes for different people. For example, your board might decide to highlight one or two of its second-level Ends as highest priority or state that second-level Ends are listed in priority order or specify percentages of available resources that will be used on each of the second-level Ends.

The deeper a board goes with respect to cost-efficiency, the more complex the choices become, so a wise board does not jump in before having thoroughly examined the possible consequences of its decisions.

HOW ENDS POLICIES LOOK

At the end of this chapter, you will find several examples of Ends policies. Notice that the way the first-level statements are constructed helps to keep everything that follows in an Ends frame because each lower-level statement is derived directly from the one above it. Also notice that Ends language in different countries will vary, not least because the nomenclature of public jurisdictions over the organizations will vary between national, regional, and local for many organizations. The examples that follow are drawn from Canada, the United States, and the United Kingdom and have been tweaked in some cases in order to better illustrate Ends design:

- A community welfare agency in Canada (Tool 5.1)
- A parks and recreation society in the United States (Tool 5.2)
- A regional library service in Canada (Tool 5.3)
- A community college in the United States (Tool 5.4)
- A public hospital in the United Kingdom (Tool 5.5)
- A closely held private corporation in Canada (Tool 5.6)

THE PROCESS OF DEVELOPING ENDS

Because Ends policies are so important, the development process needs to be a thorough one. Before your board sits down to do the hard work of drafting Ends policies, it is important that the board first do some research and development as described in the following sections.

Defining your Ends policies can have enormous implications for your organization, for it will often require facing up to issues that have been buried beneath the hurly-burly of daily activity and making choices that have never been made before. For example, the staff of a community college may find that whereas they thought they were in the business of teaching, their board has determined that they are actually in the business of producing communities with the skills, knowledge, and resources to be economically successful. Or the staff of a youth organization may find that whereas they thought they were there to organize after-school programs, the board wants them to produce child-nurturing communities. Or the managers of a small business, who thought they were expected to be highly entrepreneurial, may find that their board would rather have a steady increase in shareholder value.

As you have seen in Chapter Three, board work starts from the board's understanding of legal and moral owners' wishes, so until your board has determined what your owners want, it cannot know what your organization's Ends should be. Look back at the roots of any organization that has a board today, and you will find a group of people who came together to cause some sort of benefit for themselves. The benefit they were seeking may have been financial return, or they may have been seeking improvements for their community or their society at large. Often, perhaps increasingly, in a world in which we are all being forced to recognize our interdependence, owners may seek both financial and community benefits. Whether a board has been formed by a group of investors or by another kind of group, its job is to ensure that its organization provides the benefits for which that group created it—that is, to ensure that decisions and actions stem from the right motivation.

The changes in direction that result from Ends work can be not only hugely significant but also extremely costly. Realigning people, plans, processes, and resources is not always easy. Thus, boards need to take the planning and execution of the Ends development process extremely seriously.

Planning the Development of Ends Policies

The length of your board's Ends policy development process will depend on how much discussion your board feels it needs to engage in with its owners and around the board table before it will be able to agree on its first set of policies. Reading this chapter should give your board some idea as to what's involved, but be prepared to be flexible. Any stage can take more or less time than you think.

Some boards, especially those that meet infrequently, spread the Ends policy development process over at least a year; others attempt it over two or three meetings. Some boards do not proceed to developing their means policies until they have completed their Ends policies. Other boards begin by developing and implementing their means policies and insert a placeholder Ends policy that will be used until they have completed their Ends policy development process. Such a policy might read like this: "Whatever Ends the board has stated or implied in previous decisions or approvals will stay unchanged, pending formal adoption of Ends policies" (Carver and Carver, 2006, p. 220).Whether your board chooses to develop Ends policies before or after developing Executive Limitations policies and whatever time frame it chooses, the plan is likely to need to include the following elements.

Identifying Primary Information Needs   The information that boards need in order to begin drafting Ends policy varies, obviously. But all boards need to spend the time (usually about an hour) to do an honest appraisal of how well informed they are about the areas in the following list. I recommend that in preparation for the appraisal, individual board members review the following list and, for each item, indicate whether they feel that they are sufficiently or insufficiently informed. Performing this exercise will help your board determine what kind of information it needs to gather. Remember that ultimately it is your owners' perspective that counts and the other information is there only to help you better interpret how best to act on that perspective.

Public Policy
- Our current public policy environment
- Likely changes in our public policy environment
- Probable impact of changes in public policy on our organization

Owners' Expectations and Wishes
- What our owners—as owners—want from us now
- What our owners are likely to want from us in the future

Customers' Expectations and Wishes
- What our customers want from us now
- What our customers are likely to want from us in the future

Other

- Other knowledge about our current and future environment

Gathering Owner Input   A board can gather owner input simply by attempting to think its way into owners' shoes, by meeting with owners either en masse or in smaller focus groups, or through new or pre-existing surveys conducted by their own or other organizations. In other words, as John Carver (2006, p. 204) has suggested, owner input can be gathered by the following methods:

- *Attitudinally:* requires board members to have sufficient understanding of a large portion of their owners to be able to put themselves in their shoes
- *Personally:* requires board members to engage face to face with representative groups of owners
- *Statistically:* requires board members to gather data from surveys of owners

Whatever approach or combination of approaches your board takes to get owner input, it needs to set the right context and ask good questions as discussed in the section on building good owner relations in Chapter Three, starting on page 55. Discussing the following issues may help to get your board members thinking about how best to go about getting input from your organization's owners.

- In what setting are our owners most likely to feel comfortable interacting with us?
- What are likely to be our owners' expectations and thoughts before they interact with us?
- What questions can we ask that will produce owner rather than customer input?
- How will we handle customer input?
- What do we need to explain before, during, and after the interaction about
  - Our board?
  - How we see ownership?
  - The relationship we seek with our owners?
  - Our purpose in having this particular interaction?

Many tools and techniques for interacting with owners are available. Some are listed in Chapter Three; others appear in the following sections.

Gathering Expert Input from Staff, Board Members, and Others   Especially if they have previously been the main leadership of your organization, staff may be nervous about how the board's Ends policy development process will go. In particular, they may worry that the board does not know enough to make sensible decisions. These fears are quite understandable. They can and should be overcome by engaging the staff and the CEO in giving input on Ends policy. Staff can be particularly useful in helping the board to understand what is currently going on in the organization and the range of possible impacts of various value choices. As long as everyone understands that Ends policies must start from the board's interpretations of what owners want and be informed by what is already so, rather than the other way round, nothing but good can come of staff involvement.

Individual board members may have particular knowledge or expertise that could be useful in helping the board explore what its Ends should be. Other outside expertise in the form of papers, talks, or other consultations may also be useful. When used to inform the board as a whole, such input should help to ensure that the board is better able to fulfill its role as an informed body of owner representatives.

Gathering Input from Other Boards   As your board starts to think about creating Ends policies, it will want to be very aware of other organizations operating in your field and how your Ends may be affected by what those organizations are or are not committed to producing. Unfortunately, unless those boards also use Policy Governance and have developed their own Ends policies, that commitment may be hard to discern.

Scanning Your Environment   Digesting and summing up all the information gathered from the aforementioned sources is usually best done through full board discussion, with staff involvement. This process of reviewing your organization's internal and external worlds, or environment, is often called *environmental scanning*. The purpose of environmental scanning is for your board to get a comprehensive picture of your organization's current and potential place in the world before embarking on creating its future. Context is decisive. Your board members' mutual understanding of the past, current, and likely future social, economic, and political forces affecting your organization will be a huge influence (though not necessarily the determining influence) on the Ends policies that your board will create. Here are some questions that might help to get all the main points on the table:

Environmental Scanning Questions

- What do we know about our public policy environment that we need to take into account in envisioning our organization's future?
- What do we know about our owners' expectations and wishes that we need to take into account in envisioning our organization's future?
- What do we know about our current customers' expectations and wishes that we need to take into account in envisioning our organization's future?
- What else do we need to take into account in envisioning our organization's future (for example, funding possibilities and constraints, other organizations' work)?

Visioning and Brainstorming   Now comes what for many of your board members will be the most exciting part of their job: envisioning the future. At this point, having grounded themselves in the realities of the environmental scan, board members will probably feel it is important to give themselves permission to have an "anything goes" kind of conversation in order to free up everyone's creativity. The board can always moderate the wild ideas later, but it can't consider ideas that never make it onto the table.

Techniques for visioning range from simple activities that board members can try on their own to formal approaches that are facilitated by professional consultants. How your board members approach this task will depend on what feels comfortable and what kind of resources they feel are appropriate to devote to it. You will find descriptions of various visioning techniques in Tool 5.7 at the end of this chapter.

Drafting Ends Policies

Once your board members have had enough discussion to feel that they can start to answer the three Ends questions (What difference do we want to make? For which people? With what level of cost-efficiency?), the board is ready to start drafting its Ends policy.

Drafting anything as a group can be a challenge. Usually, the best approach is to focus on agreeing on key concepts as a group but to delegate the wordsmithing to someone else. Later, that person can bring the polished policy back to the board for further discussion and approval. As with all policies under Policy Governance, when your board sets out to draft your Ends policies, it should use the general format presented on pages 83–84 in the previous chapter. A version of that format that applies specifically to Ends policies is outlined here:

1. Create a one- or two-sentence Ends policy that states your interpretation of your owners' full intent in terms of the following questions:

   a. What difference do you want to make?

   b. For which people?

   c. With what level of cost-efficiency?

2. Consider which terms within your overall policy you need to define more specifically by creating further containers within the policy you produced in step 1.

3. Create a one-sentence policy that creates a more specific definition for each of those terms.

4. Repeat steps 2 and 3 until your board feels that it can responsibly accept any reasonable interpretation of what it has said.

Some examples of Ends policies that were created by using these steps are presented at the end of the chapter (see Tools 5.1–5.6). Following is some guidance on a few interrelated issues that may come up as your board drafts its Ends policies.

Defining the Length of Your Vision Your board's overall vision is likely to be for the long term—ten, fifteen, twenty years or even further into the future. However, your Ends policies can just state your board's vision as answers to the three Ends questions without setting a time frame. Your board is authorizing your CEO to make any reasonable interpretation of its policy, so unless the board specifies a time frame, your CEO may do so. Nonetheless, in order to create clear CEO accountability for progress toward your board's long-term vision, the board will probably want to bring its Ends policies down to a more specific level with a shorter time frame. For example, a twenty-year vision for an organization that advocates for people with disabilities might lead to an overall Ends statement such as "All people with disabilities in our community have realistic options for independent living." To bring its accountability down to a more immediate, practical level, the organization's board might proceed to create a lower-level Ends statement such as "By [*date five years hence*], people with disabilities in our community will have agreement with all relevant bodies on a plan for all to have realistic options for independent living within the next twenty years. This plan will have been arrived at in a manner that represents good value for money."

Notice that if the policy had said that the organization existed to "do planning" or "be planners," it would not have been an Ends statement because it would have specified activities instead of results. However, saying that the organization exists to produce a specific plan for specific persons with a specific cost-efficiency is an Ends statement.

Ensuring That Ends Are Feasible   A consideration that is very closely related to time frame is feasibility. Obviously, it is important that your Ends be feasible for your organization, but your board should be careful not to sell your owners short. Ends are not about improving on what you've got but rather about deciding on where you want to be. Once your board has decided where your organization wants to be, it may find that it needs to adjust its Ends to take account of where your organization is today, but its Ends do not have to be defined by where your organization is today.

Addressing Ambitions That Go Beyond What Your Organization Can Achieve   Your board may find that its overall vision goes beyond what can realistically be accomplished by your organization alone. If this is the case, for the sake of accountability, your board would be wise to bring its Ends policy down to a level that enables it to hold your CEO accountable for your organization's particular contribution to the overall vision. Your organization's wider ambitions can still be pursued at the board level through dialogue about its overall vision with the boards of other relevant organizations. For example, if your organization provides community care services for sufferers of a particular disease, your board might initially identify your organization's overall vision as a world without that disease. The board now has a choice: either it can extend the scope of your organization's work to encompass all that might be required to accomplish that broad goal, or it can stick to creating Ends policies that address community care and create a plan for dialoguing about your organization's overall vision with other organizations that can produce the other components that would be needed to achieve that vision, such as research knowledge and medical care.

Similar questions arise for the boards of organizations at the heart of federations. If the members of the federation are autonomous, the central body's Ends should be about what it can uniquely add to the whole—for example, conditions for member body success, a unified national and international image, a common vision, and informed legislation. Notice that if the local bodies were subsidiaries of the federation, its Ends would be about the fulfillment of its own vision rather than about enabling the local bodies to create and fulfill theirs.

Where to Include Your Beliefs and Philosophy   Because your Ends need to be kept in the realm of feasibility over a foreseeable amount of time and need to reflect a reasonable level of ambition, your board members may find themselves wondering how to express the philosophy, beliefs, and overall vision that lie behind their Ends policies or, indeed, everything the board does and doesn't do. The answer is to keep beliefs and philosophy out of Ends policies (which should be confined to instructions to your CEO about what benefits you require to be made for whom and with what cost-efficiency) and put them in Governance Process policies as foundational statements of your board's commitment. Examples of such statements include "We believe that all human beings should be treated with dignity" and "We are committed to a world that works for everyone." These are not statements that create any meaningful accountability (because they are not specific about who is accountable for what), but they do tell your owners and subsequent board members about where the board was coming from as it developed all of its policies, which do create meaningful accountability.

Keeping Ends and Means Clear   It is essential not to stray into means when creating Ends. Considering the term *means* in its common usage, it is easy to become confused by the fact that all lower-level Ends are means to the levels above them. The way to keep matters straight is to ask the following question: "Are we defining the difference we want to make, the people for whom we want to make that difference, or the level of cost-efficiency with which we want that difference to be achieved?" If your answer is yes, you are talking about Ends. If your answer is no, you have strayed into talking about means. The checklist in Table 5.1 will help your board to keep its Ends statements on track.

Table 5.1
Ends Policy Checklist

ENDS STATEMENTS DESCRIBE . . .	ENDS STATEMENTS DO NOT DESCRIBE . . .
The impact our owners want us to have in the world	Our organization
What we are for	What we do
The reason for our organization's existence	Keeping our organization going for its own sake
Effects	Effort, trying
Outcomes	Activities, methods, practices, procedures
Precisely what the board is holding itself and the CEO accountable for producing	What the board and the CEO will do along the way
Value added	Continuing doing what we are doing
The full scope of our ambition	Ambitions that exceed our foreseeable grasp
Destination	Direction (for example, "reduce," "raise," "increase," "improve")
Achievement	Tasks

ENDS STATEMENTS ARE . . .	ENDS STATEMENTS ARE NOT . . .
Brief	Empty words
Accurate delegation instructions	About looking good (for example, "to be the leading . . . ")

Agreeing on Ends Policy

Your board might be able to agree on the first draft of its Ends policy on the spot in the first meeting at which it is discussed, or the board's discussion might need to go to a subsequent meeting, possibly after having had an individual or a smaller group do some wordsmithing on the policy. It might even take several drafts for your board get to a policy that all can agree on. On one hand, getting something so important right is much more important than the speed at which it happens. After all, you existed without Ends policies before, so carrying on as you were for a while longer will not mean the end of the world. On the other hand, it is important to remember that while your CEO needs you to keep your direction as consistent as possible in order to maximize your organization's ability to achieve your organization's Ends, your board always retains the ability to change those Ends.

Controversy   Do not worry if your board's Ends policies prove to be controversial. Controversy is an asset to a board, for it proves that diversity is at work. If there is no controversy, it probably means that your board's ownership linkage is lacking. Controversy and confusion are not problematic as long as the board is arguing about things that matter. Arguing about things that matter is what owners want boards for. To argue about things that don't matter or not to argue at all is to shortchange your owners.

Knowing When to Stop   Do not worry if at first your board's Ends policies are shorter than you feel they may one day become. As I discussed earlier in the chapter, the further the board drills down, the more complex the issues become, and good Ends policy development takes time. Better to stay broad but accurate for the time being than to go to more specific levels before your board is ready. Chapter Seven will show you how even the broadest Ends statement gets translated into concrete measurable goals through the board's monitoring process. Also, keep in mind that even the broadest Ends statement will be a vast improvement on the non-Ends language you had before.

Monitoring Ends Policy

We all say that we want goals and that we want to evaluate our progress toward achieving them. Turning your goals into Ends expressed as results for specific people at a specific worth automatically causes them to become measurable through the Ends monitoring process. Chapter Seven provides much more information about Ends monitoring, which, in brief, works as follows:

Action	Responsible Party
1. Creation of Ends policy	Board
2. Interpretation of Ends policy (including measurable definitions)	CEO
3. Strategic planning and action	CEO
4. Production of monitoring data	CEO or other specified person or persons in light of CEO's interpretations in step 2
5. Assessment of interpretations and data	Board

Reviewing Ends Policy

You will need to schedule time on your board's calendar (see Tool 8.8 at the end of Chapter Eight) for a regular review of your Ends policies, to ensure that they remain as relevant as possible. Most boards conduct such a review annually.

Knowing That You Have the Right Ends Policy for Your Board

Let's assume that you are a board member who is really committed to your organization's making a difference. You will know that your Ends policies are right for your board when (1) you see them as describing the fulfillment of your owners' aspirations and therefore your own aspirations as their representative, and (2) you find yourself longing to make them happen. Once agreed on, your Ends should be the continual centerpiece of the board's involvement and therefore the main focus and inspiration of everyone's work. The right Ends are the ones that have you saying "that's us" or "that's what we're all about."

MOVING ON

This chapter described how to develop Ends policies. The next chapter explains how to develop all the other policies—that is, all the policies that deal with means rather than Ends.

TOOLS

TOOL 5.1 ENDS POLICY FOR A COMMUNITY WELFARE AGENCY IN CANADA

xxxxx [*name of agency*] exists so that first- and second-generation newcomers to this country make a successful transition to life in our region that justifies the funds invested to achieve it.

1. First- and second-generation newcomers will have the support they need to create an economically viable life, including

- The information and skills needed to find or create employment, including

  - The language skills needed to find or create employment

2. First- and second-generation newcomers will have the support they need to live a socially viable life, including the language, information, and skills they need to:

- Maintain a healthy lifestyle in the context of this country

- Keep themselves from physical and emotional harm stemming from their experiences before or after arrival in this country

- Be successful parents

- Maintain and expand their social support networks in the context of this country

- Obtain the support they need to sustain themselves physically, emotionally, and spiritually in later life

TOOL 5.2   ENDS POLICY FOR A PARKS AND RECREATION SOCIETY IN THE U.S.

E-1 Purpose and Outcome

The xxxx Parks and Recreation Society exists for the cost-effective achievement of members' professional success. [*This society is for parks and recreation professionals.*]

E-2 Public Policy Conditions

Members benefit from public policy conditions favorable to their professional success.

A. Legislators have reasonable acquaintance with member issues with respect to pending desirable legislation.

B. Members are knowledgeable of the status of legislative issues, with priority given to issues of substantial importance to the profession.

C. Members are knowledgeable of the political process for advancing professional success

D. Members are knowledgeable of the methods available to communicate the value of parks and recreation to local and regional decision makers.

E-3 Member Competency

Members have the skills and knowledge needed for professional leadership.

A. Members demonstrate and articulate the role of parks and recreation in creating community.

B. Members set trends in the profession.

C. Members build coalitions to increase resources.

D. Members advance within the parks and recreation profession.

E. Members communicate with decision makers at both a regional and local level.

TOOL 5.3   ENDS POLICY FOR A REGIONAL LIBRARY SERVICE IN CANADA

The people of xxx, as represented by the minister with jurisdiction for public libraries, will have equitable access to library services at a cost-efficiency no less than other similar systems.

1. Libraries will be equipped to deliver equitable access.

    1.1. There will be a network for equitable access to worldwide library collections.

    1.2. Libraries will provide services according to minimum standards.

        1.2.1. Libraries will have a mechanism for collaboration on the development and achievement of common standards.

2. The minister will be equipped to deliver equitable access.

    2.1. The minister will have expert, credible information and advice about the sector.

    2.2. The minister will have a mechanism for delivery of core information and services that need to reach all libraries.

TOOL 5.4 ENDS POLICY FOR A COMMUNITY COLLEGE IN THE U.S.

xxx College exists so that the people and communities of xxx County are equipped with the vision and skills to create or contribute to a sustainable economic environment at a justifiable cost

1. Communities have the leadership and educational resources to generate and sustain economic-base jobs.

2. Communities have the leadership and educational resources to generate and sustain a vibrant social and cultural life.

3. Students seeking transfer to universities have the qualifications to make a successful transition.

4. Job seekers have the qualifications, skills, and abilities to make a successful transition to a career or move to the next career or educational level of their choice.

5. Adults in lifelong learning programs have affordable access to a variety of high-quality learning opportunities and instructional formats.

TOOL 5.5 ENDS POLICY FOR A PUBLIC HOSPITAL IN THE U.K.

1.0 Ends

xxx Hospital NHS Trust exists so that people presenting to us achieve the best possible health outcomes at a justifiable level of cost-efficiency.

1.1 Diagnosis

People presenting to us have their condition diagnosed accurately, speedily, and safely.

1.2 Care Management

People have their care managed speedily, fully, and safely.

1.2.1 Dignity in Dying

People who are facing death have appropriate physical, emotional, and spiritual support.

1.3 Health Maintenance

All the people we serve have appropriate information, tools, and services for the promotion and maintenance of their health.

TOOL 5.6   ENDS POLICY OF A CLOSELY HELD PRIVATE CORPORATION IN CANADA

Our company exists to provide us with a return on our investment of financial, human, and relational capital that make that investment worthwhile to us.

1. We will have the satisfaction of making a difference for customers who can benefit from what we have to offer.

2. The worth of our company and therefore the worth of our shares will multiply x times over the next three years.

3. We will have had the opportunity to work for ourselves at something we enjoy.

4. We will have the benefit of working with enthusiastic, committed partners of our choice.

TOOL 5.7   VISIONING TECHNIQUES

Some of the techniques in this list are specifically designed to help your board envision the future. Others are simply designed to help make your board's underlying values explicit.

Create Your Organization's Story

As a full board, with input from the persons who have been around the longest, create a visual timeline of your organization's history, showing key events from the past. When the timeline of past events is complete, ask board members to pair up and create some alternative futures, projecting the timeline ten to fifteen years ahead. Have each pair report and then have the full board discuss which future they find most attractive and why.

Read All About It!

You are having breakfast twenty years from now on a nice sunny day, and you pick up the newspaper. What does the headline say about your organization?

Scenario Development

Create contrasting scenarios for your organization's future—for example,

- Your organization gets a huge injection of funds without any strings attached.
- Your organization's income is reduced by 75 percent as a result of some unforeseen disaster.
- Your board membership falls below the number needed for a quorum, and you cannot find any new board members.
- A top-notch advertising company offers you its services free of charge for the next five years.

In each case, consider

- What would you want to do?
- What would you actually do?
- Why?

Picture This

Ask board members to create a picture of the future they would like to see. They can draw, paint, collage—anything goes.

Mind Mapping

Mind Maps® is a trademark that belongs to The Buzan Organisation. Mind Maps are a quick and easy way to sum up a lot of interrelated information. Try breaking the board into small groups and brainstorming benefits, beneficiaries, and cost-efficiency statements, then putting them all together in a Mind Map and seeing what comes up. There are now many Web sites offering tools for creating Mind Maps. The Web site of the inventor, Tony Buzan, can be found at http://buzanworld.com.

Future Search

Future Search is a well-honed process for planning and conducting large-scale meetings that involve a wide variety of people in envisioning a desired future. They meet for sixteen hours spread across three days. People tell stories about their past, present, and desired future. Through dialogue, they discover their common ground and make concrete action plans. You can find out more by going to the Web site of the Future Search Network at http://www.futuresearch.net/method/applications/index.cfm.

Why, Why, Why?

If you keep asking "Why do we do that?" you will eventually start to uncover your Ends.

Cardstorming

Initially, board members respond to a particular question individually. Small groups of three or four are formed, and participants share individual ideas, recording the group's ideas on 4" × 6" index cards. The cards are then spread around the room and sorted, clustered, and categorized by small groups (either the original or newly formed groups) or, depending on the size of the full group, with all participants. The process can take forty-five to ninety minutes, depending on the size of the group. Cardstorming is a good technique for helping a diverse group to think creatively together in a transparent way.

How Can You Govern How Your Ends Are Achieved?

Creating Means Policies

We titled our book Let Go to Grow *because letting go is the key management and cultural shift necessary to grow, to become a firm that combines speed, flexibility, adaptability, coordination, collaboration, and innovation.*

Linda Sanford with Dave Taylor, *Let Go to Grow: Escaping the Commodity Trap*

In the preceding chapter, you saw that Ends policies define three things: what specific difference your owners want your organization to make, for whom, and with what cost-efficiency. Going back to our analogy of bike riding, it would seem that once your organization has those Ends—that is, once you know where you want to go—you should be able to jump onto your bike and head off to your destination by the fastest route possible.

The problem, of course, is that if you are really nervous about falling off your bike, you may never really get going, so in order for you to be persuaded to swap a walker's level of control for a cyclist's level of velocity, you need to have found your balance.

113

In Policy Governance, that translates to setting forth in written policies how you want to control the manner in which your organization moves toward its destination.

Once you have read this chapter, you should:

- Understand how your board can use the Policy Governance system to balance its need for organizational velocity with its need for control
- Be able to identify all the lower-level policy containers your board might want to create for controlling CEO and board means
- Be equipped to create your means policies

THE MEANS CONTROL CONTAINERS

As I discussed in Chapter Four, in the Policy Governance system, the term *means* encompasses all issues that are not about Ends. Thus, this chapter gives you more in-depth information about how your board can use the Policy Governance system to control all the aspects of your organization that are not automatically controlled by ensuring that it is accomplishing what it is for.

Remember that there are three policy containers left to fill, and all of them relate to means. The three remaining types of policies are (1) Governance Process, (2) Board-Management Delegation, and (3) Executive Limitations. The first two containers are for policies that control how the board itself can operate—that is, the means it can use. The third policy container, Executive Limitations, is for policies that control the means used by the board's delegate, typically the CEO.

This chapter covers a lot of ground, for here we will populate the remaining three policy containers we learned about in Chapter Four, starting with the two that govern the board's means, Governance Process and Board-Management Delegation, and ending with the container that governs the CEO's means, Executive Limitations. Please note that all the policy language that follows is based on templates that originally appeared in books such as *Reinventing Your Board: A Step-by-Step Guide to Implementing Policy Governance* (Carver and Carver, 2006) (see page 176 in Chapter Eight) and are also available through trained Policy Governance consultants (see page 181 in Chapter Eight).

CREATING POLICIES FOR CONTROLLING THE BOARD'S MEANS

In this section, we will be looking at the two containers for controlling your board's means: Governance Process and Board-Management Delegation.

The purpose of the policies in the Governance Process container is to control everything about the way your board conducts business between itself and its owners and business among board members. Governance Process policy is the place to talk about your board's commitments to being owners' representative and ensuring your organization's success and safety, as well as how your board is going to organize its meetings, ensure board members' good behavior, authorize the board chair or CGO and other board officers, and so forth.

The purpose of the policies in the Board-Management Delegation container is to control (1) how your board is going to delegate its authority (and to whom) in order to fulfill its Ends policies within its Executive Limitations policies and (2) how your board is going to monitor whether that authority is being properly used.

Remembering that the policies in each policy container must start with the board's broadest possible expression of owners' concerns, it may not be surprising that the initial statements in the two board means containers seem pretty universal and maybe even rather bland. However, these global statements are in fact highly meaningful, for they are all-encompassing and therefore leave no possible concern outside of your board's control and monitoring. Thus, most boards end up with a broadest policy in their Governance Process container that simply connects its authority to its owners and states its overall purpose, something like this:

> On behalf of its legal and moral ownership, the board shall ensure that [*name of organization*] achieves appropriate results for appropriate persons with appropriate cost-efficiency.

The broadest policy in the Board-Management Delegation container is typically a statement that makes it clear to whom the board is delegating organizational operation, such as this one:

> The board's sole official connection to the operational organization, its achievements, and its conduct shall be through a chief executive officer.

Your board can choose to create its own policies in each container, using the process set out on pages 83–84 in Chapter Four, or it may wish to start from the draft wording presented in the templates available through relevant books or qualified consultants (see Resources section). Whichever route your board takes, it will be important to recognize that each lower-level policy is a further definition or interpretation of the one at the level above, just as in Ends policies. Creating their own policies from scratch is an enormous challenge, and your board members should think carefully before taking it on. The advantage in doing so is that your board would completely own its policies; the disadvantage is that your board could run out of steam before it completes its policies. And, when it comes to the means policies, most boards' concerns are very similar, so why bother reinventing the wheel?

Policies in the Governance Process Container

Let us work on developing the policies for the Governance Process container first using the process set out on pages 83–84 in Chapter Four. In Table 6.1, you will find a listing of possible containers from the broadest level of policy to the narrowest. Keep in mind that these are suggestions, not prescriptions. It is up to your board to develop containers that are a good fit for your organization. This sample, however, will help you understand how policies move from broadest to narrowest, which I will discuss further.

Table 6.1
Containers for Governance Process Policies

2	**GOVERNANCE PROCESS**
2.1	**Governing Style**
2.1.1	Ends Context
2.1.2	Group Responsibility
2.1.3	Written Policies
2.1.4	Board Discipline
2.1.5	Board Development
2.1.5.1	*Orientation of New Board Members*
2.1.6	Fulfillment of Commitments
2.2	**Board Job Description**
2.2.1	Ownership-to-Organization Link
2.2.2	Written Governing Policies
2.2.2.1	*Ends*
2.2.2.2	*Executive Limitations*
2.2.2.3	*Governance Process*
2.2.2.4	*Board–Executive Function Relationship*
2.2.3	Organizational Performance
2.3	**Agenda Planning**

Source: Thanks to Ray Tooley, OurBoardroom Technologies Inc. (www.ourboardroom.com).

Let's begin with the broadest policy statement—the one that was presented in the preceding section:

> 2 On behalf of its legal and moral ownership, the board shall ensure that [*name of organization*] achieves appropriate results for appropriate persons with appropriate cost-efficiency.

This statement, being the broadest in the Governance Process category, is on the first level in this container. On the assumption that the board has chosen to number each of the four main policy categories as (1) Ends, (2) Governance Process, (3) Board-Management Delegation, and (4) Executive Limitations, Table 6.1 labels the first level in the Governance Process category "2 Governance Process. " You can use whatever numbering system works for your board as long as the difference between each of the four categories and the hierarchy of policies within each category are clear.

As I stated earlier, the policies that come under this broadest Governance Process statement, "2 Governance Process," will specify the way that the board is committed to organizing itself in a range of areas such as agenda planning, the role of the CGO, and self-evaluation. These policies are at the second level. In Table 6.1, you will notice that the first container on the second level, "Governing Style," is numbered 2.1, and that the last, "Governance Evaluation," is numbered 2.10. Within each container, there may be further levels of policy—narrower or more specific definitions of the preceding level of policy. For example, let's look at how the policies in container 2.4, which specifies the role of the CGO, might turn out. Here is an example of a second-level policy to define the chairperson's role:

> 2.4 The chief governance officer (CGO), a specially empowered member of the board, ensures the integrity of the board's process

Going to the third level might involve further specifying what the board means in terms of the results they expect from the CGO in ensuring "the integrity of the board's process." The board might create a policy container 2.4.1 to specify that assigned result:

Accordingly:

> 2.4.1 The assigned result of the CGO's job is that the board behaves consistently with its own rules and those legitimately imposed upon it from outside the organization.

Going to the fourth level might involve further specifying "its own rules," creating three further containers to specify rules on meeting content, information to be avoided, and deliberation criteria:

> 2.4.1.1 Meeting discussion content will be on the issues that, according to board policy, clearly belong to the board to decide or monitor.
>
> 2.4.1.2 Information that is for neither monitoring performance nor board decisions will be avoided or minimized and always noted as such.

2.4.1.3 Deliberation will be fair, open, and thorough but also timely, orderly, and kept to the point.

Going back up to container 2.4, the board might want to go on to create a more specific policy container 2.4.2 and containers within that to define the nature of the CGO's authority:

2.4.2 The authority of the CGO consists in making decisions that fall within topics covered by board policies on Governance Process and Board-Management Delegation, with the exception of (a) employment and termination of the CEO and (b) areas where the board specifically delegates portions of its authority to others. The CGO is authorized to use any reasonable interpretation of the provisions in these policies.

2.4.2.1 The CGO is empowered to chair board meetings with all the commonly accepted powers of that position, such as ruling and recognizing.

2.4.2.2 The CGO has no authority to make decisions about policies created by the board. Therefore, the CGO has no authority to supervise or direct the CEO.

2.4.2.3 The CGO may represent the board to outside parties in announcing the board's stated positions and in stating CGO decisions and interpretations within the area delegated to her or him.

2.4.2.4 The CGO may delegate this authority, but remains accountable for its use.

In the preceding example on the job of the CGO, the board has only gone to a fourth-level policy container. Your board members could certainly create more containers at the fourth level or even below if they so chose. However, you may be interested to know that the vast majority of boards go no further than a fourth level. Also, remember that at whatever level your board stops creating policy, your CGO is free to operate within any reasonable interpretation of what the board has said. No doubt, there will be further policies; it is just that they will be created by your CGO instead of your board as the CGO goes about the business of interpreting and thus further refining your board's policies. Thus, there is no need to cover any eventuality that your board is happy to leave up to its CGO within any reasonable interpretation of what the board has already said. And remember that your board will have to monitor every policy that it produces and that monitoring will take time and effort on everyone's part. This means that your board will want to make sure that it doesn't create policies that are more detailed than they need to be. Your board has an obligation to control everything to the extent that it feels it must on behalf of your owners, but it also has an obligation to them to avoid creating unnecessary work. Your board needs to find the right balance.

Board-Management Delegation Container

Now let us turn to the other major policy container where we put policies outlining board means. Again, let us start from the broadest level of policy in your Board-Management Delegation container, using the example from page 115, and let us assume that you have decided to number all the policies in the Board-Management Delegation so that they start with the number 3 (see Table 6.2).

Table 6.2

Containers for Board-Management Delegation Policies

3	**BOARD-CEO RELATIONSHIP**
3.1	**Delegation of Executive Authority**
3.1.1	Board Direction to the CEO
3.1.2	CEO Authority
3.1.3	Board and CEO Domains
3.2	**Monitoring Executive Performance**
3.2.1	Purpose of Monitoring
3.2.1.1	*Report Distribution*
3.2.2	Policy Monitoring
3.2.3	Monitoring Frequency
3.2.4	CEO Evaluation
3.2.5	Noncompliance Remediation
3.2.6	Monitoring Schedule
3.3	**Executive Compensation**
3.3.1	Organizational Performance
3.3.2	Compensation
3.3.3	Compensation Aims
3.3.4	Annual Compensation Assessment
3.3.5	Additional Compensation

Source: Thanks to Ray Tooley, OurBoardroom Technologies Inc. (www.ourboardroom.com).

Here is the first-level template policy defining the board-CEO relationship:

> 3 The board's sole official connection to the operational organization, its achievements, and its conduct shall be through a chief executive officer (CEO).

This time we will work through an example, moving to two lower levels of the container. First, let us assume that you want to specify the official delegation to the CEO. Note that in Table 6.2, this specification is shown as a second-level policy statement and numbered 3.1. The statement might read as follows:

> 3.1 Only officially passed motions of the board are binding on the CEO.

Next, going to a further level of specificity about official instructions might result in the following third-level policies:

> 3.1.1 Decisions or instructions of individual board members, officers, or committees are not binding on the CEO except in rare instances when the board has specifically authorized such exercise of authority.
>
> 3.1.2 In cases when board members or committees request information or assistance without board authorization, the CEO may refuse any such requests that are disruptive or that require, in the CEO's opinion, a material amount of staff time or funds.

Again, your board could go to further levels of specificity and create more containers than are shown in Table 6.2. My warnings about overdoing your policymaking apply here, too. Again, you need to find the right balance between too much control and too little control. But the beauty of using the Policy Governance system is that the level of control you have chosen to exercise will never be none, for starting at the broadest level first means that you have always exercised control at least at that level.

CREATING POLICIES FOR CONTROLLING THE CEO'S MEANS

In its policies about board means, the board is talking to itself and its CGO, officers, and committees about how it will govern. Now we are moving on to the section of policy in which the board talks to its CEO about how he or she should manage. My discussion of these policies will look a little different from the discussion earlier in this chapter. I will discuss how your board needs to think about and shape these policies before I begin the discussion on filling the containers.

Charging the CEO with Accomplishing Ends

Your organization does not exist to have staff or services or technology; your organization exists to make certain people's lives different in a certain way with a certain cost-efficiency. In other words, your organization exists to fulfill its Ends. Governing for velocity requires governing in such a manner that Ends are achieved as fully and quickly as possible.

The best way for your board to control the efficiency of your CEO's means is to clearly and consistently demand that your Ends be accomplished, for unless you add in other considerations, if your CEO is being held accountable for accomplishing Ends, he or she will automatically align everything the organization does to accomplish those Ends as efficiently as possible.

To illustrate the point, imagine that I am your personal chef and that you have given me a multitude of ingredients and told me that you want some biscuits. I will use my ingredients to produce biscuits. However, if you tell me you want a cake, you will get a cake but it will be whatever kind of cake I choose. However, if you tell me you want a chocolate cake, that is precisely what you will get. In other words, by specifying your Ends, you are automatically controlling my means. And assuming that you have employed me because of my culinary skills, which you are regularly testing, and assuming that I am free to get whatever help I might need, you would be much better advised, if you want to use your time efficiently, to let me get on with it rather than try to interfere beyond what is essential to your requirements.

The conundrum for your board is that it understandably wants and, in many cases, needs to go beyond simply charging the CEO with the task of achieving Ends. Going back to my chocolate cake, what would happen if I made a big mess in the kitchen or hired way too many sous chefs to help? Clearly, the board needs to exercise some additional control over means. But how much control and of what sort? These are critical questions. Remember that whenever the board gets involved in specifying your CEO's means, it is adding to the cost of Ends production and the cost of monitoring. Every requirement you put on me as a chef about how I should produce the cake (rather than what the end product should be) will slow me down and create another item that you need to check up on in order to make sure that I am following your instructions. Switching back to the bike analogy, every limitation we encounter will cause us to put the brakes on, to swerve, or to delay forward motion in some other way. In other words, every limitation, or non-Ends expectation, that we introduce defeats our purpose to some extent. Thus, it is vital that your board keep its involvement in your CEO's means to the minimum necessary. Otherwise, velocity will be lost, and the value of having learned to ride the Policy Governance bike will be lost as well.

And there's more. Even if you have board members who have a great deal of skill and expertise in the areas that the CEO has to manage, if your board allows itself to be drawn into making management decisions, it will have lost its ability to hold the CEO accountable for the results and slowed the organization down to the board's decision-making pace. Governance and management are two different jobs. One is about defining and ensuring owners' collective best interests; the other is about fulfillment. Each job must be performed to its full potential if all the parts of an organization are to be aligned in pursuit of a clearly defined vision of success. Collapsing the two jobs into one means that it is impossible to tell whether either job is being done properly.

So where does this leave boards in creating policies to control CEO means? Charging a CEO with accomplishing Ends is the first step, but it clearly isn't enough. Boards need a way to find an appropriate level of control, one that doesn't interfere with the CEO's work. This is where Executive Limitations policies come in.

Telling the CEO What He or She *Cannot* Do

As we have already seen, from the board's perspective, organizational velocity is achieved not by dictating means but by holding the CEO accountable for accomplishing Ends and leaving the maximum possible freedom for executive action.

Policies in the Executive Limitations container therefore need to control your CEO's means choices in a manner that

- Enables your board and CEO to see exactly what freedom is and is not available

- Reflects a balance between owners' needs for velocity and control

Freedom Through Prohibition

Giving your CEO freedom through prohibition in Policy Governance means telling your CEO what he or she cannot do rather than what to do.

It is interesting to note that freedom through prohibition is also a concept that is important in law. According to the *Stanford Encyclopaedia of Philosophy*, "It is probably a practical necessity that every legal system has an unwritten 'closure' rule to the effect that whatever is not prohibited is permitted" (Campbell, 2005). This is the principle on which Executive Limitations in the Policy Governance system are based; Executive Limitations—instructions given to the CEO about means—are always stated in terms of what the CEO can't do.

The contrariness of Executive Limitations policies may give rise to some controversy. Some people fear that such negative language sounds dictatorial and will be seen as offensive by their CEO and staff. These fears can usually be allayed by your CEO, who is likely to point out that the staff welcomes clear direction from the board and finds the message "Everything is permitted unless it is forbidden," along with knowledge of exactly what is forbidden, highly empowering rather than disempowering.

The other common objection to the negative language convention is that prohibition, which designates the boundary between what is acceptable and unacceptable, can be just as clearly stated positively as negatively. It is possible to argue that saying "Do not cause or allow anything that is illegal" has exactly the same effect as saying "Cause or allow only what is legal." Saying "Do not allow significant assets to be uninsured" may be seen as having exactly the same effect as saying "Ensure that our significant assets are insured."

However, it is *very strongly* recommended that your board use the negative language convention because

- It will act as a constant reminder to your board that the purpose of Executive Limitations policy is not to tell your CEO which means to use but, rather, which to avoid.

- It helps to reinforce the board's message to your CEO that everything is permitted unless it is forbidden.

- It requires deeper thought to define what needs to be avoided rather than simply reel off a string of instructions, which helps to ensure that policies embody the viewpoint of external owners rather than internal staff members.

In any case, what matters is that the board define the boundary between acceptable and unacceptable means in such a way that the board and the CEO can clearly see it.

Deciding What to Prohibit at the Broadest Level   As we move into the discussion of what to prohibit, it will be useful to consult Table 6.3, which outlines possible containers for Executive Limitations policies. In order to balance velocity with control, every policy in every container shown must

- Seek to limit the range of freedom within which the CEO can make means choices (in order to exclude those the board would consider unethical or imprudent) rather than dictate particular choices

- Be a more specific interpretation of the policy in the larger container within which it sits

---

Table 6.3
Containers for Executive Limitations Policies

4	**EXECUTIVE LIMITATIONS**
4.1	**Emergency Executive Succession**
4.2	**Protection of Assets**
4.2.1	Insurance
4.2.2	Maintenance of Assets
4.2.3	Exposure to Liability Claims
4.2.4	Purchase Limits
4.2.4.1	*Conflict of Interest Protection*
4.2.4.2	*Comparative Price Limits*
4.2.5	Controls on Funds
4.2.6	Document Safekeeping
4.2.7	Intellectual Property Protection
4.2.8	Credibility and Public Image
4.3	**Financial Planning**
4.3.1	Credible Projections
4.3.2	Expenditure of Funds
4.3.3	Unacceptable Conditions
4.3.4	Board Funding
4.3.5	Fiscal Soundness
4.3.5.1	*Future Deficits*
4.3.5.2	*Reserves*

(Continued)

Table 6.3
Containers for Executive Limitations Policies (continued)

4.4	**Financial Management**
4.4.1	Asset-Liability Ratio
4.4.2	Debt Limitations
4.4.3	Debt Settlement
4.4.4	Government Payments
4.4.4.1	*Government Register*
4.4.5	Pursuit of Receivables
4.4.6	Long-Term Reserves
4.4.7	Purchase Limits
4.4.8	Borrowing Limits
4.4.9	Expense Checks
4.5	**Communication and Support to the Board**
4.5.1	Material News
4.5.2	Monitoring Data
4.5.3	Board Policy Compliance
4.5.4	Information Support for the Board
4.5.5	Information Criteria
4.5.6	Noncompliance Reporting
4.5.7	Integrity of Communications
4.5.8	Administrative Support for the Board
4.6	**Treatment of Staff, Volunteers, and Contractors**
4.6.1	Employment
4.6.2	Personnel Rules
4.6.3	Protections
4.6.4	Concerns
4.7	**Treatment of Customers or Clients**
4.7.1	Privacy
4.7.2	Information
4.7.3	Complaints

Source: Thanks to Ray Tooley, OurBoardroom Technologies Inc. (www.ourboardroom.com).

Before we begin the work of defining what is prohibited, let's step back and look at what has already been said about the CEO's role through board-management delegation policies. Assuming that the board has stated in these policies that the CEO is being charged with nothing less than the fulfillment of its Ends policies, and assuming that the board is monitoring the extent to which their CEO is indeed fulfilling the Ends, board members now need to ask themselves, What else matters? The answer, briefly stated, is that what matters is that the organization is safe—that the integrity of the owners' asset is protected in terms of ethics and prudence. The way that your board can ensure that everything is protected at some level is to create a global policy in the Executive Limitations container that reads something like this:

> The CEO shall not cause or allow any organizational practice, activity, decision, or circumstance that is either imprudent or unethical.

Prohibiting imprudence clearly covers all kinds of risks at the broadest level. For example, no reasonable interpretation of such a prohibition could allow the CEO to act illegally or put the organization in the way of financial harm. Prohibiting unethical behavior or circumstance also covers many matters that would be regarded as unethical by your organization's owners or by the society in which your organization operates. Your board may want to just use this language, or it may want to adjust the language somewhat to make it more explicit—for example, by adding phrases such as "or in violation of commonly accepted business and professional practices."

Deciding What to Prohibit at Lower Levels   To decide on your policy containers at the second level, you need to expand on the process shown on pages 83–84 in Chapter Four by answering three important questions.

The first and most fundamental question is "What are the main areas in which lack of ethics or imprudence could arise in our organization?" For example, your board might decide that finance and treatment of staff are the most likely problem areas. The areas that your board decides on will be the second-level policy containers. Notice that in Table 6.3, there are seven areas at the second level, ranging from protection of assets to treatment of customers. The areas that your board decides to include will depend on the particular features of your organization.

Next, in each of the second-level areas, your board needs to consider the following question: "What is the range of possible interpretations left open by the broadest level of Executive Limitations policy?" To answer this question, it may help for the board to ask some what-if questions to test some scenarios. For example, let's say that your organization has a second-level policy on treatment of staff that reads as follows:

> With respect to the treatment of paid and volunteer staff, the CEO shall not cause or allow conditions that are unfair, undignified, disorganized, or unclear.

Now, let's try some what-if questions. What if the staff were threatening to go on strike? Would this policy, along with the broadest Executive Limitation that prohibits imprudent and unethical behavior, sufficiently protect the organization? What if a staff member had a heart attack? If your board concluded that your organization was covered well enough from the consequences in the first scenario but not the second, it might add a more specific policy at the next level—for example,

> The CEO shall not allow staff to be unprepared to deal with emergency situations.

Finally, your board needs to ask "In the range of possible interpretations that our policy leaves open, are there any that our CEO could demonstrate to be reasonable that are unacceptable to the board?" If so, your board will wish to make it clear that such interpretations are prohibited by further narrowing their policy at the next level. For example, going back to the second-level policy on treatment of staff that reads "With respect to the treatment of paid and volunteer staff, the CEO shall not cause or allow conditions that are unfair, undignified, disorganized, or unclear," what interpretations could be made that could be justified as reasonable but still be unacceptable to the board? Could the CEO dismiss someone according to the legal definition of unfair dismissal? Clearly, no. Could the CEO force someone to work without knowing what is expected of them? Clearly, no. But could the CEO fail to give written instructions on personnel rules? Unlikely, but possible; hence, your board might wish to create a more specific container or policy area within which it might say something like this:

> The CEO shall not operate without written personnel rules that (a) clarify rules for staff, (b) provide for effective handling of grievances, and (c) protect against wrongful conditions such as nepotism and grossly preferential treatment for personal reasons.

As with everything your board does, the acid test for whether to prohibit a particular type of means should not be your board members' personal preferences but your board members' interpretation of owners' best interests. Clearly, from the viewpoint of ownership, there are some means that could be very efficient in producing Ends but that would still be unacceptable to your board. To judge whether your board can justifiably declare some means unacceptable, try applying the following tests:

The Ethical Test

If your board believes that your ownership would be willing to forgo accomplishment of Ends rather than compromise a particular ethical standard, it should exclude the breach of that standard from your CEO's range of allowable means choices.

The Prudential Test

If your board believes that failure to impose a particular restriction on your CEO's range of means would create an unacceptable risk to the fulfillment of your owners' Ends, due to of loss or harm to owners' Ends-producing asset (your organization), it should impose that restriction.

More on Ethics Ethics is an enormous and complex subject. Board control, however, must be unambiguous. A board cannot be half accountable. For the sake of organizing your board's values, it is probably simplest to treat matters of ethics at the board level as absolute rather than situational and therefore to take the position that achieving your Ends can never justify the use of unethical means. In other words, if your organization normally plays by the rules but resorts to fiddling with the accounts when the organization's survival is on the line, it cannot be said to be behaving ethically. For the board to justify prohibiting the CEO from doing something for ethical reasons, it has to be convinced that its owners would rather forgo *any* accomplishment of Ends rather than compromise that ethical standard.

Your board's ethical standards will not necessarily be the same as another board's. For example, if you are on the board of an organization with the End of "people living free from alcohol addiction," you might take the stand that you would be willing to forgo any accomplishment of Ends rather than accept money from companies associated with the promotion of alcohol sales. Another board might regard such an association as an issue of prudential risk but be willing to take the risk. Yet another board—for example, the board of a corporation that designs restaurants—might regard the possibility of such an association as entirely positive and therefore not something that the board needs to speak to at all.

More on Prudence In contrast to controlling ethics, controlling prudence will require your board to decide where it sits on the continuum from saying

"Don't even get out of bed" to saying "Risk everything." The board's only way of legitimizing where it chooses to place itself on that continuum is, again, its interpretation of its owners' best interests. In seeking to understand owners' best interests, what the board is really seeking is the right balance between the risk of leaving the owners' asset vulnerable to harm and the risk of having the asset be unproductive. In other words, using the asset inevitably involves risk, but *not* using it also involves risk.

The extent to which your organization should be insured is a decision resulting, in part, from a risk-reward calculation. The same goes for deciding whether to change an organization's name or otherwise substantially alter its identity, use a particular management technique, or employ a new administrative assistant. Ditto for almost every management choice. Risk, however trivial, must always be factored into your staff's decisions, even if it's only a matter of weighing the cost of doing something versus the cost of doing nothing. Thus, if your board were to try to eliminate all management discretion in regard to risk, nothing would get done.

When your board decides that it needs to adopt an Executive Limitations policy on the grounds of prudence, it must do so because it believes that its owners would regard the level of risk otherwise involved as intolerable.

Crafting Lower-Level Executive Limitations Policies   The preceding discussion, along with the examples in Table 6.3, should help your board think through what further containers it might need to organize its policies. Remember that we have already created a powerful broad-level policy that prohibits anything that would fall outside any reasonable interpretation of *ethical* or *prudent*. Given that a Policy Governance board regularly and rigorously monitors its policies (see Chapter Seven), if your board enacts just this one policy, your organization is already covered across the whole range of matters that would clearly breach those standards and thus your board needs to make sure that there is a real necessity for anything further that it adds. Clearly, it would be imprudent (even if under certain circumstances, it could reasonably be claimed to be ethical) to do anything unlawful. Clearly, it would be unethical (even if under certain circumstances, it could reasonably be claimed to be prudent) to verbally abuse your staff. So the broad policy that we developed earlier already offers an organization quite a bit of protection. This fact is important to keep in mind as your board goes about creating and filling containers. Here, again, is the global Executive Limitations policy statement, which would correspond to the first level in Table 6.3:

4 The CEO shall not cause or allow any organizational practice, activity, decision, or circumstance that is either imprudent or unethical.

You will notice that seven second-level containers are shown in Table 6.3. In the "Emergency Executive Succession" container, the board has made just one second-level policy provision and left all further interpretation up to its CEO, whereas in the "Protection of Assets" and "Financial Planning" containers, the board has created three levels of policy, getting ever more specific as it adds levels.

As an example, let us take Policy 4.5 from Table 6.3, titled "Communication and Support to the Board." The first question is, "What more, if anything, even assuming it is reasonably interpreted, does the board need to add to global policy 4 to define what it cannot live without in terms of communication or support from its CEO?" Clearly, the more demanding is the communication or support the board demands from its CEO, the less time the organization will be able to spend on fulfilling the owners' desire for Ends production. Equally clear, there is a level of ignorance that the board would feel it could not tolerate without inviting undue risk on behalf of its owners. It's a balance—and a balance that, short of the owners themselves, only the board has the right to determine.

In the template example, the assumption is that the board has decided that it does need to add further specification as follows:

> 4.5 The CEO shall not permit the board to be uninformed or unsupported in its work.

And now let us assume that the board decides that it needs to move to a third level of specificity, further defining the range within which they are willing to accept any reasonable interpretation of being uninformed and unsupported. The board might say:

> Further, without limiting the scope of the foregoing by this enumeration, he or she shall not:
> 4.5.1 Let the board be unaware of relevant trends, anticipated adverse media coverage, threatened or pending lawsuits, and material external and internal changes, particularly changes in the assumptions on which any board policy has previously been established.

4.5.2 Neglect to submit monitoring data required by the board (see policy on Monitoring CEO Performance) in a timely, accurate, and understandable fashion, directly addressing provisions of board policies being monitored.

4.5.3 Let the board be unaware of an actual or anticipated noncompliance with any policy of the board.

Moving to a fourth level of specificity, the board might want to be clear that it would not accept an interpretation of 4.5.3 that excluded the CEO's opinion on the board's behavior and state:

4.5.3.1 Actual or anticipated noncompliance includes the CEO's opinion on board compliance with its Governance Process and Board-Management Delegation policies, particularly in the case of board behavior that is detrimental to the work relationship between the board and the CEO.

Your board could create more third-level policies as shown in Table 6.3 or further levels of specificity and more containers than are shown in Table 6.3. My warnings about overdoing policymaking apply here too. You need to find the right balance between too much control and too little control. The beauty of using the Policy Governance system is that the level of control you have chosen to exercise will never be none, for starting at the broadest level first means that you have always exercised control at least at that level.

To labor the point, the value of starting from the top in every policy container is that so much can be encompassed in so few words. And notice that what is being encompassed at every level in Executive Limitations is not only all your known risks but also all your unknown risks, which is extremely fortunate, given that, as David Hillson points out, our "risk radar," however well attuned to what's going on, can see only a limited way into the future, and many risks do not emerge until or unless other things happen (Hillson, 2005).

I am sure that the following language did not pass you by: "Further, without limiting the scope of the foregoing by this enumeration, he or she shall not . . ." The purpose of these words is to allow the board to indicate that the lower-level statements are not necessarily a comprehensive interpretation of the next highest-level statement. After all, the point of the higher-level statements is to encompass as much as possible. There are two alternatives. First, if the board does mean to restrict the interpretation of the upper-level statement through the lower-level statements, it can indicate that intent by saying something like this:

> The full scope of the foregoing statement is defined in the following:

Second, it can create one policy within the Board-Management Delegation section that says something like this:

> The sum of Ends or Executive Limitations at any policy level may be taken as defining the full scope of the policy at the foregoing level, but only if justified by the CEO to the board's satisfaction.

Steering, Not Rowing

Remember that in creating lower-level Executive Limitations, it is very easy to slip into specifying how your CEO should do the job and that this is to be avoided if your board wishes to maintain the organizational velocity that Policy Governance is designed to foster. In particular, Executive Limitations should not be used to compensate for an unfit CEO, a subject covered further on pages 144, 145, and 156 in Chapter Seven and page 173 in Chapter Eight. And beware the vast array of advice in books, on Web sites, and from consultants about what boards should and should not be controlling in terms of CEO means. Some of this information may be useful to your board, but it will need to tread carefully, for it can easily fall back into specifying means rather than controlling them through prohibition.

Take, for example, the handling of matters that can create personal liabilities for board members, such as the payment of taxes and wages. Certainly, it is an excellent idea for board members to make sure that they

- Are fully educated about their liability
- Have appropriate liability insurance
- Have control over the matters concerned

The way to go about this, however, is not to jump into the details of managing payroll but to create and regularly monitor Executive Limitations policies that govern the organization's financial condition, including prohibiting late filing of government-required payments, perhaps with the addition of a policy such as this one:

The CEO shall not cause or allow board members to be uninformed about nor unnecessarily exposed to personal liability in the course of their work.

The board might also want to create a more specific policy at the next level, such as this one:

Board members' liability insurance shall not be allowed to fall below that recommended by [*name of appropriate professional body*].

We all enjoy feeling helpful to someone, and telling someone how to do their job rather than what to achieve and what to avoid seems a good option. But notice what happens. "Don't operate without a personnel manual" tells your CEO that he or she must have a personnel manual. But saying "Don't allow staff to be ignorant of personnel rules" gives the CEO a full range of choice on how to accomplish what the board has asked for and gives the board what it really wants. In the end, what the board cares about is the result—a staff that knows the rules—and if your CEO can provide something better that achieves the same result, your board and your owners will be that much the happier.

Always remember that your board's aim, as far as possible, should be to control the range of freedom within which your CEO makes choices about means rather than to directly make particular choices. In other words, your board's aim should be to steer your organizational boat rather than to row it.

However, your board will inevitably need to make some choices about means—potentially, any of the choices that your policies forbid your CEO to make. Therefore, it is completely pointless to add "except with board approval" to any policy, for that proviso automatically applies to every single Executive Limitation. For example, if your board has prohibited your CEO from reducing reserves, it does not mean that reserves cannot be reduced; it means that such a decision would have to be made by the board. But notice that when and if such a decision does come to the board, it would still make complete sense for the board to make it based on its Ends and Executive Limitations criteria, for if the board has done its job in creating those policies, what other criteria could there be?

Whatever the level at which your board stops creating policy, your CEO is free to operate within any reasonable interpretation of what the board has said; thus, your CEO will, no doubt, be creating further policy. Again, there is no need for your board to cover any eventuality that it is happy to leave up to your CEO, within any reasonable interpretation of what it has already said. And never forget the cost of monitoring and therefore your obligation to control as much as possible in as few words as possible.

Dealing with External Requirements   In creating its policies, your board will naturally need to take account of whatever constraints are imposed on your organization by outside authorities, be they statutory or regulatory, as well as the requirements of relevant codes of good governance that your organization wishes to observe and your organization's own founding documentation, including bylaws. However, taking account of what others require of your organization does not necessarily mean taking their words at face value (for more on this topic, see pages 45–52 in Chapter Three). Remember that most policies and laws are open to some range of interpretation. Your job is to interpret the requirements that you are obliged to fulfill in a manner that will satisfy the body that is doing the requiring *and* that is in your owners' best interests.

In some instances, your board may find itself ostensibly obliged to make decisions that clearly are best made by your CEO, according to your policies. In these cases, you can adopt the practice of placing required approvals on the board's agenda, as explained on page 174 in Chapter Eight.

KEEPING YOUR POLICIES ALIVE

As the primary tools for steering an organization, policies are alive and real in the life of Policy Governance organizations every day. In Chapter Eight I will go into this concept in more detail, explaining how to deal with concerns about your organization as they arise. In this vein, I will also address annual policy reviews in Chapter Eight.

For now, I want to leave you with a thought. The entire Policy Governance system is about cascading levels of empowerment from society to owners to board to CEO to staff. This recognition of hierarchy is not an endorsement of a heavy-handed management style—far from it. It is about freeing people up by giving them clear spans of control appropriate to the needs of their respective jobs.

MOVING ON

This chapter has covered a lot of ground. Indeed, it has covered everything about policy development except Ends, which were dealt with in Chapter Five.

This chapter and the preceding one together provide a proactive, comprehensive, and integrated policy framework that we can use to clearly classify and organize all of a board's governance concerns.

Now we will move on to the final piece of the system: policy monitoring, the method by which your board will make sure that its policies are having the desired effect.

How Can You Keep Your Board Accountable?

Monitoring Your Policies

The single major challenge addressed by corporate governance is how to grant managers enormous discretionary power over the conduct of the business while holding them accountable for the use of that power.

Robert Monks and Nell Minow, *Corporate Governance*

Creating policies that specify the difference that owners want your organization to make (your Ends) and controlling all that goes into making that difference (your means) has been our mission for the last two chapters. If your board has completed that work, it should be the proud possessor of a comprehensive set of shared policies that form the context for board and CEO accountability.

Now we are going to install the last piece of the Policy Governance system: policy monitoring and evaluation. This is the piece that makes all the policies count, for it is through monitoring and evaluation that your board will be able to demonstrate that it is exercising proper oversight and that it is accountable for everything that goes on in your organization.

Once you have read this chapter, you should understand

- How board accountability relates to monitoring and evaluation
- The principles that underlie monitoring and evaluation in Policy Governance
- How to conduct effective monitoring and evaluation

BOARD ACCOUNTABILITY

Boards need to delegate management of their organization to someone. In very small organizations, that someone can be other board members, but usually it will be a CEO. In any case, board members need to delegate to each other in order to ensure the smooth running of their board. But whatever they may delegate to whom, boards remain accountable for what happens next. Being accountable can be defined as being obliged to account for, explain, and justify one's acts or omissions. Legally, boards are obliged to account to their owners and the societies in which they operate for compliance with their bylaws and with the law of the land and for fulfillment of their duty of care. Morally, boards are also obliged to account to their owners for everything pertaining to the use of the organization.

Specifically, in order to ensure that they are fully accountable and can avoid any potential trouble, boards need to be able to show that they (1) are legally compliant, (2) are loyal to the best interests of their organization, (3) are sufficiently well-informed, and (4) have demonstrated a level of care that might be reasonably expected of a member of that type of organization. Not only do boards need to be clear about how they are governing, why they are governing that way, and how well they are doing, but they also need to be able to prove it. Without Policy Governance, the audit trail for board accountability comes down to examining the minutes of board meetings to see how individual issues are or are not handled. With Policy Governance, a rich audit trail for board accountability is provided by the board's policies and by the monitoring and evaluation of those policies, which we will explore in great detail in this chapter. If you are interested, however, in more detail about how Policy Governance helps ensure accountability in the four areas identified at the beginning of this paragraph, see Tools 7.1 to 7.4 at the end of this chapter.

Notice that in Tool 7.2, I have interpreted loyalty to the organization as loyalty to owners. The loyalty duty makes sense only if it means loyalty to the owners of the organization. It is hard to see how the interests of an organization can supersede the interests of the people who have the right to dispose of it entirely should they see fit.

Monitoring Is Where Accountability Begins

In Policy Governance, accountability begins with creating expectations in the form of policies, but it isn't fulfilled until your board can answer questions like "How do you know whether your CEO is achieving the Ends you have put forth in your Ends policies or whether he or she is operating within the stated Executive Limitations?" and "Is your board following the processes outlined in your Governance Process policies?" Monitoring is the way that your board will go about answering these questions. Your board has a variety of choices about how to conduct the monitoring process, but the results must be that your board gets regular and credible reassurance that its delegates are (1) making reasonable interpretations of its policies and (2) operating in accordance with those interpretations.

Delegating for Accountability

For the monitoring process to truly provide accountability, it is essential that the board be clear about who is accountable for the fulfillment of its expectations, as set out in its policies. And it is important that the fulfillment of the board's expectations be delegated to someone who has the authority and the capacity to fulfill them.

Clarity   Typically, boards delegate to two persons, their CEO and their CGO. In Policy Governance, the board's expectations for the CEO are set out in its Ends and Executive Limitations policies and its expectation of the CGO is that he or she will ensure the board's compliance with its Governance Process and Board-Management Delegation policies. Thus, unlike governance schemes in which the CGO may also act as CEO, in Policy Governance, each of the board's delegates has a distinct domain. In each of these domains, it is essential that accountability be clear. Should your board wish to distribute accountability for Ends and Executive Limitations to more than one person or body—that is, divide up the work of the CEO in some fashion—clarity will be undermined and therefore the accountability of all parties will be compromised to some degree. It is certainly possible for boards using Policy Governance to delegate to persons or committees that perform parts of rather than the entire CEO role. However, if a board delegates the CEO role to multiple parties, the board either has to see itself as the CEO or have its delegates stand or fall together for accountability purposes.

Authority   Whomever your board makes accountable for fulfilling its expectations must also have the requisite authority. Having authority means that that person will be solely responsible, for when you delegate responsibility for parts of the same job to more than one person, responsibility for the *whole* job stays with you. Alternatively, when you directly delegate all aspects of one job to one person, you can hold that person fully accountable for the whole job, which, given that you remain accountable for anything you delegate anyway, is where you want to be.

I sometimes illustrate this point by asking one board member in a workshop to think of himself or herself as my assistant whom I have charged with getting some flower arrangements set up in the reception area of my office. Then I ask the rest of the board two questions:

"Is my assistant now responsible for all aspects of the flower arrangements?"

"Is my assistant now fully accountable to me for the flower arrangements?"

They typically answer yes.

Then I inform my board member assistant whom I had previously charged with beautifying the reception area, "By the way, I asked the receptionist to purchase the flowers."

Finally I return to the whole board and ask:

"Is my assistant now responsible for the flower arrangements?"

"Is my assistant now fully accountable to me for the flower arrangements?"

"If my assistant is not fully accountable to me for the flower arrangements, who is accountable for the flower arrangements now?"

They generally answer no to the first two questions, and in answer to the third question, they generally say, "You are." which enables me to bring out the following points in subsequent discussion:

- When you directly delegate responsibility for parts of the same job to more than one person, accountability for the job as a whole stays with you.

- When you directly delegate all aspects of one job to one person, you can hold that person fully accountable for the job (even if that person delegates further).

- How did my assistant feel about the introduction of the receptionist into the picture? Relieved? Annoyed? What does that tell us about getting the best from people?

Capacity   There is no point in delegating to someone who does not have the capacity to meet your expectations; doing so will inevitably lead to unnecessary grief for all. Obviously, all boards should work hard to get CGOs and CEOs who are equipped to do their job, but be warned that because the jobs are so clear in Policy Governance, it will quickly become obvious if your organization doesn't have people who are up to the board's requirements. See pages 156 in Chapter Seven and 169 and 173 in Chapter Eight for more on your board's options in such a case.

FUNDAMENTALS OF THE MONITORING PROCESS

Once your board has created policies and delegated their fulfillment, it is ready to develop a process for monitoring. Typically, this process involves specifying what types of reports the board needs to see in order to verify compliance with policies and then outlining a schedule or an approach for reviewing the reports. In other words, as a Policy Governance board, your board will be able to demonstrate that it has defined what constitutes relevant information and that it regularly acquires such information. This includes information that ensures performance against its criteria through the disclosure of interpretations and data.

Demonstrating due care, whatever jurisdiction you are in, is likely to mean showing that you have given serious attention or consideration to the avoidance of damage, risk, or error that a reasonable person in similar circumstances would.

How Often Should the Board Get Reports?

For every policy that your board creates, its members need to decide on the frequency with which they wish to assure themselves that their standard is being met. In making this decision, the board needs to take into account the fact that it will take delegates a considerable amount of time to produce a good monitoring report and that is time that could instead be used to produce the results the board seeks. The cost of monitoring needs to constitute a reasonable proportion of both the board's and the staff's overall expenditure of time and effort.

Most boards seem to stick with reviewing most policies annually but monitoring policies that control finances quarterly. Once these dates are agreed on, they should be placed on your board's calendar, as shown in Chapter Eight.

Who Should Do the Reporting?

There are essentially three reporting choices for each policy that your board monitors: delegates, a third party, or board members.

Delegates   Your board can have your delegates, usually your CEO and CGO, produce monitoring reports regarding the respective domains for which they are accountable. This option is what boards using Policy Governance traditionally call an *internal report*. Your CEO may have staff help draft reports on your Ends and Executive Limitations policies, and your CGO may have fellow board members help draft reports on your Governance Process and Board-Management Delegation policies, but the CEO or CGO remains accountable for their entire content.

A Third Party   Your board can require your delegates to give their policy interpretations and data to a suitably qualified external person or group, who will then produce the final report to the board. This option is called an *external report* or an *independent report* and is attractive because it provides a third party's assurance of the validity of the data. However, it is an expensive option if your board has to pay for the help. One suggestion is to intersperse internal reports with external or independent reports on a random or less frequent basis—perhaps every three years—for a few key policies. Most boards stick mainly to internal reports for all policies except those that it makes sense to refer to their official financial auditor.

Board Members   For policies for which the board itself already has the data, the board members can decide that they will ask the accountable delegate for his or her interpretation but produce the data themselves. Of course, this means that the board must be in a position to vouch for policy compliance or not. For policies for which the CEO is accountable, this option would only be available if the policy required the CEO to provide direct support to the board in some way or another. However, this option could apply to all of the policies for which the

CGO is accountable, for the board directly witnesses their implementation. This option is called a *direct board report.*

What Should the Reports Look Like?

Tool 7.5 shows a typical format of an Executive Limitations Report. The full meaning of some of the terms in this report will be explained as you read this chapter. This format gives the board introductory summary data for ease of reference, including some history on the status of previous reports.

How Should the Reports Be Reviewed?

It is vital that your board review each monitoring report thoroughly, to establish whether it is clear about the extent to which its policy is or is not being implemented. Again, there are a few choices for the review process:

1. Each board member can review monitoring reports as soon as they are produced and communicate their conclusions to the CGO. The CGO can then report everyone's conclusions at the next board meeting and ensure discussion of any concerns that arise.

2. The board can review the monitoring reports as a group at the first meeting after each is due.

3. The board can do a first review as a group as in option 2 and then do an individual review and final conclusion as in option 1.

Monitoring should be kept as objective as possible; it should consist of a simple comparison between policy expectations and what is actually so for the period covered by the report. Only when your board members have made that comparison and assured themselves that their conclusions are valid can they decide on what, if anything, should be done as a result.

It may be helpful to use a questionnaire to guide board members in their review of each monitoring report. See Tool 7.6 at the end of this chapter for a sample questionnaire.

In any case, your board is likely to find it essential to have an education session on monitoring, perhaps with the help of publications such as *Reinventing Your Board* (Carver and Carver, 2006) and *Meaningful Monitoring* (Moore, 2005). Doing mock assessments of a few sample reports can help board members confirm their learning, especially if your board can get help from a trained Policy Governance consultant.

What Should the Compliance Standard Be?

To say that your organization is in compliance with a policy would commonly be taken to mean that the policy's intent has been completely fulfilled. Clearly, this is often unrealistic. Indeed, in the case of Ends policies, the day when the board's intent can be completely fulfilled is likely to be years in the future. For many Executive Limitations policies, too, compliance in the sense of complete fulfillment may be a long way off or, indeed, impossible. For example, your organization might have an Executive Limitation policy that forbids allowing staff to be unprepared to deal with emergency situations. Your CEO's interpretation of that policy might include all staff members' having knowledge of artificial respiration techniques, which, depending on the size of your staff, might not be feasible for a good while to come—or ever.

Your board could try to set compliance standards for every policy, but doing so is likely to take the board well out of its depth and into extremely difficult and even dangerous waters. The alternative is to require that when your policy does not make the compliance standard explicit, your delegate's reasonable interpretation of the policy will include addressing the standard that the delegate has set. In that case, your board members should be checking that the policy interpretations they receive indicate

- What the overall compliance standard should be
- By when that overall compliance standard should be met
- The interim standards or benchmarks that should be used as the interim compliance standards

How Should Compliance and Noncompliance Be Dealt with?

It is easy for boards to treat compliance with policies as normal and thus fail to mark it and celebrate it. Eventually, this lack of recognition may lead delegates to feel that the only time the board pays them any attention is when there is something wrong. It is a very good idea for boards to make sure that their delegates know how much they appreciate all that goes into making compliance happen.

It is also easy for boards to step over monitoring reports that either do not show compliance or do not provide them with the information they need to make clear determinations about compliance. Holding people accountable is not something that human beings find at all easy. But for board members, it is an unavoidable requirement of their job.

As part of determining your monitoring process, your board should discuss how it will handle unacceptable monitoring reports as well as monitoring reports that show noncompliance. Unacceptable monitoring reports can be dealt with by requiring that any offending reports be resubmitted with the information needed for the board to make a clear determination about whether a reasonable compliance standard has been set and met. Monitoring reports that show noncompliance can be dealt with in a number of ways, depending on the situation.

Noncompliance does not necessarily mean that your delegate is at fault. Accountability and fault are two entirely different matters. Noncompliance is simply what is so today. Why it is so today could be for any number of reasons—for example,

1. Some unforeseeable catastrophe has hit your organization that has set you back, even though your organization has good risk management planning in place.

2. The policy has been recently introduced, and it is going to take significant time to achieve full compliance.

3. Your delegate has found that compliance with this policy would create noncompliance with another policy and has therefore secured your board's agreement to be out of compliance until the conflict can be resolved.

4. Your delegate does not have the level of competence required to get the organization into compliance.

5. Your delegate is deliberately ignoring or contravening the board's policies.

Notice that situations 1, 2, and 3 can all be resolved by ensuring that your delegate makes a reasonable interpretation of what the overall compliance standard should be, by when that overall compliance standard should be met, and what interim benchmarks should be used as interim compliance standards toward the overall compliance standard. In such cases, noncompliance may continue to be reported for a while but no fault accrues to your delegate.

Dealing with incompetence or intransigence is obviously much harder and much rarer. For noncompliance in these cases, the board's action on individual monitoring reports must be to demand compliance by a specified date and follow up to ensure that they get it. Board actions in relation to overall CEO and board evaluation are examined later in this chapter.

Making Your Monitoring Process Count

Once your board agrees on its monitoring process, it is essential that the process be documented in your board's relevant policies so that your whole board and its delegates have a clear idea of what is expected of them. Typically this means having in your policies

- A board calendar that shows for each policy how frequently it is to be monitored and who is to report on it
- A definition of what a monitoring report should include
- A requirement that delegates provide monitoring information in a timely fashion that meets the board's definition of what a monitoring report should include
- A clear process for board review of monitoring reports
- A statement of the board's process in the case of noncompliance

Now, let's look more specifically at monitoring reports in each policy category. I will begin with the monitoring of Ends policies and will go into detail about how to craft reports. Because the process of creating monitoring reports for Ends policies can be used to create monitoring reports in the other three policy areas, I won't provide the same level of detail for those.

MONITORING ENDS POLICIES

Ends monitoring is hugely valuable to your organization. Not only does it ensure that the whole organization is clear about its purpose and moving toward that purpose, but it also produces lots of information that supporters, including funders and investors, find really helpful. Supporters increasingly want to measure outcomes and benefits rather than activity, and Ends monitoring data gives them just that. All in all, getting Ends monitoring right is worth it. In this section, I will point out some things to look out for when monitoring Ends. The key points of the process are summarized at the end of this chapter in Tool 7.7.

Ends Monitoring Reports Include Interpretations That Refine Ends Policies

In delegating fulfillment of Ends to your organization's CEO, along with the authority to act in accordance with any reasonable interpretation of board policy, your board is giving your CEO the power to take the relevant policies to the next level. Thus, when you see Ends interpretations in monitoring reports, they should be Ends themselves. This is crucial, for if your CEO's Ends interpretation translates Ends into means, you will inevitably find that the data is all means-based too and you will be back to being clueless about what is so in regard to your organization's level of Ends accomplishment. Take, as an example, an organization that has within its Ends policy the words "children can read." If the CEO's interpretation of those words is "the organization must create opportunities to learn," board members will likely find themselves with a lot of data about classes and curriculum but none the wiser about how many children can and cannot read. Instead, the CEO needs to produce something that looks more like a further refinement of "children can read," which might be something like "children will score in the xth percentile on statutory reading tests." Ends interpretations, therefore, must always be lower-level Ends—that is, further specifications of benefit, beneficiaries, or worth.

Ends Interpretations from the CEO Must Relate to the Whole Policy

As we saw in Chapter Five, Ends statements, like all policy statements in Policy Governance, are structured as a series of containers that each fit within a larger container. The broadest Ends container is sometimes called the *global statement*. When your CEO and staff are interpreting your organization's Ends policies, they would be wise to start with the most specific level, for as they move up to interpret broader and broader levels of statements, they will be able to see more clearly what, if anything, still remains to be interpreted at the higher levels. Eventually, on arriving at the global statement, they may find that they feel that they can give the board a credible rationale for saying something like the following:

> I believe that in stating its more specific Ends, the board has thoroughly interpreted this overall End and that therefore my interpretations of the policies at the most specific level form a complete interpretation of this overall End.

If, however, the CEO finds that some aspects of the board's global policy statement have not been taken to a second or lower level, he or she is obliged to do that interpreting unless the board makes it clear that the greater specificity provided by their lower-level policies represents their entire interpretation of the global Ends statement by including language immediately following the global Ends policy statement such as:

> Achievement of this End means the accomplishment of the following:

In my experience, when the CEO does expand on the board's interpretation of the global policy statement, the board often adopts that interpretation (or a variant on it) as its own at its next Ends policy review. That is fine as long as the board is clear that it is no longer willing to accept any reasonable interpretation of their existing language.

What Ends Monitoring Reports May Not Show

When reports are done properly, your board should be able to see how your CEO's interpretations of its Ends are driving the organization. This may well mean that your board will start to see changes in what the organization is doing. Activities that do not contribute to Ends accomplishment will fall away, and new activities that better support Ends accomplishment will get going. Ends monitoring reports should show your board where your organization is on Ends accomplishment, but they will not necessarily tell much about how that is being achieved. Thus, it is important that your board think carefully about what it needs to know, when, and why. For example, if your board is an elected board, it may be important for your members to have some knowledge of how Ends are being achieved, but it isn't a monitoring issue, just an issue of keeping yourselves informed.

What your board determines it needs to know can be put into an Executive Limitations policy governing your CEO's communication or support to the board. As long as your board is completely solid on its commitment to governing through its policy, only good can come from having your CEO keep the board in touch with significant changes. However, your policy needs to guard against board members' trying to intervene directly when they hear about something that does not meet with their approval. In Chapter Six on pages 131–132 you will find some of the kind of language your board might want to have in a policy governing the flow of information from the CEO to the board. Also in Chapter Eight, on pages 184–185, you will find some advice for board members who must deal with public concerns.

Each End Should Have Interim Benchmarks

As I pointed out in talking about compliance standards on page 144, the complete accomplishment of Ends is always somewhere in the future. Consequently, for each End, your board should expect to see an interpretation that seeks to justify not only an overall compliance standard but also one or more interim standards or benchmarks that your CEO wishes you to accept as compliance.

What Reports Should Include When There Is Little Data

When your board starts using Policy Governance, your CEO will not automatically have the data needed to demonstrate where your organization is on Ends accomplishment. Clearly, your CEO will need to get to work immediately on making interpretations and collecting data, but both of these steps will take time and are worth doing well. In the meantime, your board may need to be satisfied with rather crude indicators. This situation should not be a problem, for as John Carver often says, "a crude measure of the right thing is better than an exact measure of the wrong thing," but your board should at least be clear that your CEO is working to implement the systems that will give you a more satisfactory level of data in the future.

Monitoring Ends Policies: An Example

Let's take the example of a community college and examine a monitoring report that relates to one Ends statement in particular—the second-level statement labeled 1.1. First, the global Ends statement:

> 1. Our college exists so that the people and communities of our area are equipped with the vision and skills to create or contribute to a sustainable economic environment at a justifiable cost.

Here are the second-level statements:

> 1.1. Communities have the leadership and educational resources to generate and sustain economic-base jobs.
> 1.2. Communities have the leadership and educational resources to generate and sustain a vibrant social and cultural life.
> 1.3. Students seeking transfer to universities have the qualifications to make a successful transition.
> 1.4. Job seekers have the qualifications, skills, and abilities to make a successful transition to a career or move to the next career or educational level of their choice.

1.5. Adults in lifelong learning programs have affordable access to a variety of affordable, high-quality learning opportunities and instructional formats.

As can be seen, there are only two levels of policy. The first-level policy is labeled 1, and the second-level policies are labeled 1.1 to 1.5. Let us assume that the CEO is starting by interpreting the second-level statement labeled 1.1, which reads as follows:

Communities have the leadership and educational resources to generate and sustain economic-base jobs.

The first concept that requires interpretation is clearly the word *communities*. Who are the intended beneficiaries of this particular Ends policy? By defining *communities*, the CEO will be producing a lower-level Ends definition.

What follows is one possible reasonable interpretation. Note that the CEO has taken the trouble to justify the interpretation as "reasonable," knowing that several possible reasonable interpretations exist and that some board members might prefer that their CEO had chosen one of the alternatives.

I interpret *communities* in the case of 1.1 and all other Ends policies to mean the entire county, divided into the areas shown in the table below and on the attached map. I believe that this interpretation is reasonable because these are the communities identified by our county government for planning purposes on the basis of size, accessibility to community resources, and community identity.

The next concept that appears to require interpretation is *leadership resources*. The CEO might interpret this very simply:

I interpret *leadership resources* to mean people.

Things become a bit more complex when we move ahead to interpreting what is meant by communities having the leadership resources "to generate and sustain economic-base jobs." Note that the CEO's interpretation provides a compliance standard or operational definition and a justification.

I interpret communities having "the leadership resources to generate and sustain economic-base jobs" to mean that each community has *at least one* active body of local persons with the vision and expertise to develop economic-base jobs. I believe that this interpretation is reasonable based on the conclusions of a meeting held last month with community development specialists from our county and the three counties that have demonstrated the greatest economic growth over the last decade.

The next term to interpret is *educational resources.* This time, the CEO, believing that the reasonableness of the interpretation is unlikely to be questioned, has not sought to provide a justification.

I interpret *educational resources* to mean educational materials and programs delivered through any mechanism.

And so on to the last part of End 1.1 that needs interpreting. Again, notice that a compliance standard as well as a justification has been provided.

I interpret communities having "the educational resources to generate and sustain economic-base jobs" to mean that *all* community members have

a. Online training resources (in their own home or in their nearest educational center) for economic development and entrepreneurship

b. Online training resources (in their own home or in their nearest educational center) for developing skills appropriate to the kind of work actually available.

I believe that this interpretation is reasonable based on the conclusions of a meeting held last month with community development specialists from our county and the three counties that have demonstrated the greatest economic growth over the last decade.

Now, let's examine the data. Note that the data in Table 7.1 provide benchmarks for progress toward the overall compliance standards set in the earlier interpretations. Each of these benchmarks represents the CEO's interpretation of Ends accomplishment at that point and needs to be justified as such. Thus, the CEO needs to say something like this:

The data are directly related to each of my policy interpretations and include my interpretation of benchmarks for Ends accomplishment with complete Ends fulfillment by 2013. These benchmarks are justified as reasonable based on an analysis produced by xxx Consulting Ltd. of the minimum time needed to achieve the required realignment of our financial and human resources without putting the organization in financial or legal jeopardy.

Of course, not every organization can afford to pay for the services of external consultants. One or more volunteers with relevant expertise can also be used. The point is that for the board to be confident that they have fulfilled their responsibility to owners for assuring that the CEO's interpretations are reasonable, external verification is likely to be needed.

Finally, here is the compliance conclusion:

I report compliance as shown in Table 7.1.

Note that this is the first report on this policy, so full compliance is not projected until several years hence. However, the CEO has produced and justified

Table 7.1
Data on Communities with Educational Resources to Generate and Sustain Economic-Base Jobs

ENDS ACCOMPLISHMENT BENCHMARKS	PERCENTAGE OF COMMUNITIES WITH ACTIVE ECONOMIC DEVELOPMENT AGENCIES	PERCENTAGE OF COMMUNITY MEMBERS WITH ONLINE RESOURCES FOR ECONOMIC DEVELOPMENT OR ENTREPRENEURSHIP TRAINING		PERCENTAGE OF COMMUNITY MEMBERS WITH ONLINE TRAINING RESOURCES FOR RELEVANT WORK SKILLS	
		AT HOME	AT NEAREST EDUCATIONAL CENTER	AT HOME	AT NEAREST EDUCATIONAL CENTER
2009 (actual)	25%	10%	30%	10%	40%
2011 (projected)	50%	20%	50%	20%	60%
2013 (projected)	100%	40%	100%	40%	100%

Note: This table shows full compliance projected for 2013. Benchmarks for interim Ends accomplishment are shown in the column on the far left. Reports showing the data for each community are also attached.

as reasonable interim benchmarks for compliance and so can report compliance in 2009. Also the CEO remains free to change these benchmarks at any time between now and 2013 as long as he or she can still justify the new benchmarks as a reasonable interpretation of the board's Ends.

MONITORING EXECUTIVE LIMITATIONS POLICIES

As I mentioned earlier, the principles and practices that underlie the monitoring of Executive Limitations policies are almost exactly the same as those for monitoring Ends policies. The monitoring report for Executive Limitations policies will be crafted by the CEO and will begin with his or her further interpretations of the board's policies, just as in the Ends monitoring report. The key points in crafting Executive Limitations monitoring reports are summarized in Tool 7.8 at the end of this chapter, and you will note that they parallel the points in the summary on monitoring Ends policies. Now I will use an example to illustrate the process of monitoring Executive Limitations policies.

Monitoring Executive Limitations Policies: An Example

Let's take the example of an organization with the Limitations statement referred to earlier in this chapter:

> The CEO shall not allow staff to be unprepared to deal with emergency situations.

Let's also say that this statement is one of several that sit within a policy container called "Treatment of Staff," which, at the broadest level, states the following:

> The CEO shall not cause or allow paid or volunteer staff to work under conditions that are unfair, undignified, disorganized, or unclear.

Starting at the most specific level, the CEO might say something like:

> The board has defined staff as "paid or volunteer" (see the broadest-level Treatment of Staff policy). I interpret *paid* to mean all staff who are direct employees of our company. I interpret *volunteer* to mean all persons who donate their time to us as official members of our volunteer program. *Official* means that they have completed a Volunteer Information Sheet.

I interpret *emergency situations* to mean situations that endanger life, including medical emergencies, environmental emergencies, fire, malicious threats, and transport accidents. I interpret not allowing staff to be "unprepared to deal with emergency situations" as

a. 95 percent of staff report that they are informed about recommended actions that could preserve their lives in the event of an emergency arising in the course of their duties.

b. All senior staff (Levels 4 and above) and all volunteer managers are certified by the Red Cross as having the basic skills needed to respond to emergency situations.

c. The buildings and vehicles for which we currently have responsibility are provided with the list of equipment recommended by the relevant health and safety agency for our organization.

When the CEO uses the preceding compliance standards, the data in the monitoring report might look something like those in Table 7.2.

Finally, here is the compliance conclusion:

I report compliance as shown in Table 7.2.

Table 7.2
Data on the Emergency Preparedness of Staff

ENDS ACCOMPLISHMENT BENCHMARKS	PERCENTAGE OF STAFF AWARE OF LIFE-SAVING ACTIONS RELATED TO THEIR DUTIES	PERCENTAGE OF SENIOR STAFF AND VOLUNTEER MANAGERS CERTIFIED AS HAVING BASIC SKILLS		PERCENTAGE OF BUILDINGS AND VEHICLES WITH EMERGENCY EQUIPMENT	
		SENIOR STAFF	VOLUNTEER MANAGERS	BUILDINGS	VEHICLES
2009 (actual)	75%	50%	30%	90%	100%
2010 (projected)	95%	75%	50%	100%	100%
2011 (projected)	95%	100%	100%	100%	100%

Note: This table shows full compliance projected for 2011. Benchmarks for interim Ends achievement are shown in the column on the far left. Reports on individual work sites are also attached.

This is the first report on this policy, so full compliance is not projected until several years hence. However the CEO has produced and justified as reasonable interim benchmarks for compliance. This means that the CEO can report compliance in 2009. Also note that the CEO remains free to change these benchmarks at any time between now and 2011 as long as he or she can still justify the new benchmarks as a reasonable interpretation of the board's Ends.

CEO EVALUATION

The two areas of monitoring that we have looked at so far—Ends and Executive Limitations—provide the basic information that the board needs to evaluate the CEO. Thus, using Policy Governance, annual CEO evaluation becomes simply a matter of summarizing the results of the previous year's monitoring. As we have seen, noncompliance does not necessarily mean fault, so the board needs to review the conclusions of its monitoring report assessments rather than the CEO's compliance conclusions.

Under Policy Governance, CEO evaluation becomes a short process based on clear criteria—a marked contrast with the long and tortuous process that many CEOs must endure. Boards that are used to other kinds of CEO evaluations may get dragged off task by people who try to introduce evaluation criteria that have not been expressed in the board's policies. Certainly, the board can agree to discuss any additional concerns for future inclusion in policy, but to assess the CEO against unstated criteria would be to break the social contract between the board and the CEO.

Attaching compensation to CEO evaluation is a tricky subject. Your board would need to consider the following questions:

- Assuming that you have decided to pay a reasonable market rate for a suitable CEO, what, other than changes in the cost of living, would cause you to agree to vary that amount from year to year?

- Your board's Ends and Limitations policies are, in effect, your board's compliance standards as reasonably interpreted by your CEO; assuming that you are demanding and getting reasonable progress toward fulfilling them, what would be bonus-worthy performance?

First of all, in regard to Executive Limitations policies, given that Limitations are about avoiding things rather than achieving things, your board may well decide that satisfactory performance in terms of Limitations is a basic prerequisite of the CEO's job. In this case, poor performance on Limitations would be a cause for serious concern, but good performance would simply be expected. Awarding bonuses for exceptional Ends performance is obviously an attractive possibility, but defining *exceptional* is not easy, and all incentive schemes run the risk of encouraging employees to manipulate the truth by setting low targets and finding ways to exaggerate results. Your board should look very carefully before it decides to adopt any kind of scheme beyond payment of a good salary. Whatever your policy on CEO compensation, it fits within the Board-Management Delegation container and is open to the CGO's further interpretation.

Dealing with a CEO who is not up to the job, for whatever reason, is not easy, especially if the chances of finding a good replacement are slim. Adopting Policy Governance is likely to bring such issues to the fore because accountability becomes so much clearer and the board has to bear in mind that what it allows, it creates. In any case, your board is accountable for ensuring that your organization has a good CEO and needs to decide how to make that possible in the shortest amount of time. In the meantime, the board has several options, including

- Having a management services agency provide an interim CEO
- Having a board member act as interim CEO
- Having a staff member act as interim CEO

Inevitably, in such situations, board members may find themselves feeling that the board needs to play a bigger role in management, but it is better to make sure that the interim CEO has a range of good internal and external support than to blur the lines of accountability.

MONITORING GOVERNANCE PROCESS AND BOARD-MANAGEMENT DELEGATION POLICIES

Regularly monitoring and evaluating your board's performance against its Governance Process and Board-Management Delegation policies has a powerful and positive impact on board performance. Again, as it did with Ends and Limitations monitoring, your board needs to decide on its process, using the advice that starts on page 141. As we have already seen, the person who has the authority to make any reasonable interpretation of Governance Process and Board-Management Delegation policies is your CGO, so it makes sense to find out what that person's interpretation of the policies is as part of deciding on the monitoring process. However, your board might also decide that this inquiry is not necessary, for the CGO's work, unlike the work of the CEO, takes place in full view of the board, so the board members may be happy to rely on the evidence of their own eyes.

Typical processes for evaluating board means policies include

- Taking one of the policies at each meeting and assessing performance through full board discussion

- Assigning particular policies to particular board members and having them produce draft data and compliance conclusions according to an annual calendar

- Having the CGO produce all the reports, addressing a different policy at each meeting

- Having the CGO produce the reports but invite board members to provide input data on any instances of noncompliance that they are aware of

- Having an external consultant familiar with Policy Governance assess the board's compliance through review of board policies, agendas, and minutes

BOARD EVALUATION

Annual board evaluation can take place at three levels: whole board, board officer, and individual board member. Evaluation in each case typically takes the form of full board discussion, summing up the results of the regular policy monitoring process described in the preceding section.

For boards using Policy Governance, board evaluation means assessing themselves against their interpretation of owners' values as documented in their policies. Other board assessment schemes abound, but always bear in mind that the criteria they suggest may or may not align with your owners' expectations and that, ultimately, it's your owners' expectations that count.

In the course of board monitoring or evaluation, any issues of individual board member or board officer compliance that arise should be dealt with by the CGO, using his or her authority to implement any reasonable interpretation of applicable policy. Should any issues arise in regard to the CGO's performance, they should be dealt with by the whole board. Having a good CGO, like having a good CEO, is a crucial board responsibility.

MOVING ON

The next and final chapter fills in some of the final pieces that may be helpful in introducing the Policy Governance system, summarizes the key points from all that you have read so far, and attempts to send you on your way with high hopes and strong resolve.

TOOLS

TOOL 7.1   DEMONSTRATING LEGAL COMPLIANCE

Using the Policy Governance system, we can demonstrate legal compliance at the *board* level by showing that our board members

- Educate themselves about all legislation, regulations, and bylaws that apply to them as a board

- Explicitly state their commitment to legal compliance in their Governance Process policies

- Regularly monitor and evaluate themselves against the policy standards described above.

Using the Policy Governance system, we can demonstrate that we are acting accountably in regard to legal compliance at the *organizational* level by showing that board members

- Use their Executive Limitations policies to explicitly prohibit our CEO from causing or allowing any illegality

- Regularly monitor and evaluate our CEO against the policy standards described above

TOOL 7.2   DEMONSTRATING LOYALTY

Using the Policy Governance system, our board can demonstrate that it is acting in a manner that is loyal to the best interests of our organization at the *board* level by showing that board members

- Explicitly identify in their Governance Process policies
  - The people to whom the board holds itself ultimately accountable for that loyalty (that is, our owners)
  - How the board creates and maintains its connection with those persons
- Have a policy for resolving conflicts of interest on the board in their Governance Process policies
- Regularly monitor and evaluate themselves against the policy standards described above

Using the Policy Governance system, our board can demonstrate that it is acting in a manner that is loyal to the best interests of our organization at the *organizational* level by showing that board members

- Use their Executive Limitations policies to explicitly prohibit our CEO from causing or allowing any conflicts of interest in the operation of the organization
- Regularly monitor and evaluate our CEO against the policy standards described above

TOOL 7.3 DEMONSTRATING BEING WELL INFORMED

Using the Policy Governance system, our board can demonstrate that it is keeping itself well informed at the *board* level by showing that board members

- Have made an explicit commitment to board education in their Governance Process policies
- Have informed themselves sufficiently to develop a comprehensive set of policies that govern our board
- Have made an explicit commitment to regular review of all board policies in their Governance Process policies
- Regularly monitor and evaluate themselves against the policy standards described above

Using the Policy Governance system, our board can demonstrate that it is keeping itself well informed at the *organizational* level by showing that board members

- Have informed themselves sufficiently to develop a comprehensive set of policies that govern our organization
- Use their Executive Limitations policies to explicitly prohibit our CEO from failing to provide information for the monitoring of those policies
- Use their Executive Limitations policies to explicitly prohibit our CEO from causing or allowing the board to be uninformed about significant matters
- Use their Executive Limitations policies to explicitly prohibit our CEO from failing to notify the board in a timely fashion of any actual or anticipated noncompliance with any policy
- Regularly monitor and evaluate our CEO against the policy standards described above

 ## TOOL 7.4   DEMONSTRATING CARE

Using the Policy Governance system, our board can demonstrate that it is taking due care at *board* and *organizational* levels by showing that board members

- Have created a risk management framework by developing a comprehensive set of policies that govern the conduct of the board and the organization
- Have informed themselves sufficiently to ensure that those policies are comprehensive through adequate board education as set out in their Governance Process policies
- Have made an explicit commitment to regular review of all of their policies in their Governance Process policies
- Regularly monitor and evaluate themselves and our organization's CEO against the policy standards described above

TOOL 7.5 SAMPLE EXECUTIVE LIMITATIONS MONITORING REPORT FORMAT

CEO Monitoring Report Due:

Date Submitted:

POLICY PROVISION	INTERPRETATION	COMPLIANCE AS OF [*Date of last report*]	COMPLIANCE AS OF [*Date of current report*]
Broadest Provision	No change	**Noncompliant**	Compliant
	No change	**Noncompliant**	Compliant
	Changed	Compliant	Compliant
	No change	Compliant	Compliant
	No change	Compliant	**Not measured**

For Each Policy Provision

Policy Provision:

Interpretation, including any compliance standards and justifications:

Data related to the above:

Compliance conclusion:

TOOL 7.6 ASSESSMENT OF A MONITORING REPORT

1. Is the interpretation of the compliance standard required reasonable?

   Yes   No   Unsure

2. Is the data sufficient to establish the level of compliance?

   Yes   No   Unsure

3. Is the compliance conclusion supported by the data?

   Yes   No   Unsure

4. Does the compliance conclusion show acceptable performance?

   Yes   No   Unsure

Other comments?

 ## TOOL 7.7   KEY POINTS FOR MONITORING ENDS POLICIES

1. The CEO's interpretations of Ends policies should create justified operational definitions of each policy so that relevant data can be collected to answer the following questions:

   a. What is so now?

   b. What is a reasonable overall expectation or compliance standard?

   c. What are reasonable interim compliance standards?

2. Interpretations of Ends policies are always lower-level Ends—that is, further specifications of benefit, beneficiaries, or worth.

3. Interpretations must cover the whole policy.

4. To avoid unnecessary duplication, interpretations should be made for the most specific level of Ends before proceeding to the next broadest level.

5. The CEO's work of interpretation and data collection should commence as soon as the board's policy is created.

TOOL 7.8 KEY POINTS FOR MONITORING EXECUTIVE LIMITATIONS POLICIES

1. The CEO's interpretations of Executive Limitations policies should create justified operational definitions of each policy so that relevant data can be collected to answer the following questions:

   a. What is so now?

   b. What is a reasonable overall expectation or compliance standard?

   c. If necessary, what are reasonable interim compliance standards?

2. Interpretations must cover the whole policy.

3. To avoid unnecessary duplication, interpretations should be made for the most specific level of Limitations before proceeding to the next broadest level.

4. The CEO's work of interpretation and data collection should commence as soon as the board's policy is created.

Embarking on Policy Governance

*Participation is perhaps the surest way to inspire commitment.
Participation in planning and decision making leads to
ownership, and that in turn builds the commitment
that is a prerequisite for excellence in workmanship.*

Laura J. Spencer, *Winning Through Participation*

Having made the decision to embark on developing a new system of governance, you have entered an entirely different phase: installation. Here is where your journey begins.

Reading this chapter will help you through the process in the following areas:

- Getting your people going
- Addressing your current circumstances
- Planning and implementing your policy creation process
- Ensuring continuous development and support

GETTING YOUR PEOPLE GOING

It is people's commitment to governing for velocity that is going to make or break your success with Policy Governance. Peter Drucker has said, "Doing anything differently, let alone innovating, always creates unexpected difficulties. It demands leadership by people of high and proven ability. If those people are committed to maintaining yesterday, they are simply not available to create tomorrow" (Drucker, 1999).

Your Board's Job

The most important aspect of getting your people going is getting them going in the right direction, which means being very clear what the board's job is and having that description set out in your Governance Process policies. As with all other job descriptions, accountability is best served when work is described in terms of its desired products rather than activities. The Policy Governance board's job, as set out in a Governance Process policy, would be something like this:

Board Job Description

Specific job outputs of the board, as an informed agent of the ownership, are those that ensure appropriate organizational performance. Accordingly, the board has direct responsibility to create:

1. The link between the ownership and the operational organization

2. Written governing policies which address the broadest levels of all organizational decisions and situations

   a. Ends: Organizational products, impacts, benefits, outcomes, recipients, and their relative worth (what good for which recipients with what cost efficiency)

   b. Executive Limitations: Constraints on executive authority that establish the prudence and ethics boundaries within which all executive activity and decisions must take place

   c. Governance Process: Specification of how the board conceives, carries out, and monitors its own task

d. Board-Management Delegation: How power is delegated and its proper use monitored; the CEO role, authority, and accountability

3. Assurance of successful organizational performance

In addition your board members may choose to commit themselves to producing some nongoverning products, such as a certain quantity of funds or a certain type of public policy or fair hearing of particular arbitration cases. In taking on such additional work, the board should be clear that it has the capacity to do so *without* sacrificing the quality of its governance products.

In my experience, this consideration can be painful when it comes to fundraising. I see many CEOs deeply frustrated that their board is not doing more to help with fundraising and many boards floundering for lack of clear commitment and direction. The board must be clear: Is it committing to raise a certain amount under its own direction? Is it requiring its members to give a certain amount of individual volunteer help under the CEO's direction? Or is it leaving fundraising entirely to the CEO, who can still ask individual board members for help even though the board has not compelled them to respond?

Your Board Members

As your board embarks on Policy Governance, it is important to consider whether the board's composition is right for its new job description. How your board is currently composed may well reflect your board's current worldview. In other words, if your board has seen itself as the CEO's helper, then your board will have members who are happy to play that role. They may be experts in particular aspects of the CEO's role, such as technology or human resources. They may be CEOs themselves. They may have great connections for raising funds or making political inroads. Alternatively, if your board has seen itself primarily as a watchdog, its membership is likely to include several people with accounting and legal backgrounds. If, however, your board has seen itself primarily as a forum in which to compete for resources for various constituent groups, the board will be a group of advocates. And if your board has seen itself as getting things done, it will be made up of people who take pride in getting on with doing things. In other words, a board's composition tends to reflect the conscious or unconscious assumptions of those who elect or appoint its members, and the kind of governance they get is the result of those assumptions.

Boards that use Policy Governance need people who are interested in governing for velocity, and that means people who are willing to come at their work from the perspective of ownership rather than management. To be on a Policy Governance board, you do not have to attempt to be as expert as the CEO in human resources or information technology or any other management arena, and you do not need to have to have great connections or deep pockets. Undoubtedly, your organization might be in need of such resources, but the board's job is first of all to govern. Management and fundraising resources can be obtained from others. Governance can only be provided by the board.

If the membership of your board includes people with executive responsibilities, you will need to consider how to handle the inevitable conflicts of interest that arise. As a Policy Governance board, you will clearly distinguish governance from management, and the impossibility of playing both roles simultaneously will become very apparent. Here is an example of some language on conflict of interest from a Governance Process policy on the role of board members created by the board of a hospital that, by law, includes its CEO and several other executives on the board:

1. Board members are jointly accountable to the ownership of xxx for proper governance of xxx.

   1.1 All board members, executive and nonexecutive, are responsible for participating in governance on behalf of the ownership, not in management on behalf of management, when acting as board members.

      1.1.1 In considering matters where there is a clear and unavoidable Conflict of Interest between their executive and board roles, executive directors are required to absent themselves from discussion.

The policy then goes on to enumerate the particular conflicts that apply in their organization, including the appointment and removal of the CEO, CEO remuneration, and consideration of CEO monitoring reports.

The Role of the CGO in Making the Transition to Policy Governance Once you have implemented Policy Governance, the CGO's role can be summarized as keeping a group of equals—the board—to its word—the board's policies. As such, the CGO's role plays a critical part in the board's continuing operation of Policy

Governance: ensuring that the board is constantly reminded of its policy commitments and either adhering to or altering those policies but never ignoring them. On page 118 in Chapter Six, you will find some language you might want to use as a basis for describing the role of your CGO.

Your CGO is also likely to be very influential in the lead-up to implementing Policy Governance but not necessarily the deciding influence. CGOs who have seen their role as being the CEO's boss or have otherwise wielded a great deal of personal power may not take easily to the kind of servant-leadership required of the CGOs of Policy Governance boards. In such cases, the board as a whole has to decide what it wants and, if necessary, find a new CGO. One suggestion that can help everyone concerned is to have discussions about whether to adopt the Policy Governance system facilitated by someone who is not the CGO, thereby freeing up both the board and CGO for a full and frank exchange of views. The most important part of this conversation is for the board to speak up. Ultimately almost every CGO has to recognize that his or her authority is subject to the board's majority will. I say "almost every CGO," for there are rare instances in which a board's by-laws state that the CGO shall be appointed by the legal ownership rather than by the board. In such situations, having a CGO who opposes the board's adoption of the Policy Governance system can force the issue that only the ownership can answer. Do they regard the CGO or the board as accountable for governance? As I have already noted, there is no such thing as half-accountability.

Ideal Qualities of Board Members   In Chapter Two on page 21, I described the typical perspectives and competencies possessed by board members who are comfortable using the Policy Governance system.

In addition, your board may want to seek specific qualities that will help enrich its policy discussions. Because the board is standing in for diverse owners, it is a very good idea to have that diversity reflected on the board. Other good reasons for having a diverse board include setting a good example in your community and seeding future board leadership. It is also useful to have people who have a good understanding of the wider environment in which the organization is seeking to make a difference and who are able to impart wisdom about how the board as a whole should go about communicating with owners in different communities. The board may even wish to ask board members who have knowledge of particular communities to spearhead the board's communications with owners in those communities. However, if your board is going to be a governing body rather than a forum for deciding among the competing claims of customer groups, it is vital that all board members understand that they are *all* required to approach *all* their policy decisions from the best interests of *all* their owners.

So what does your board do about current board members who find that the board's adoption of the Policy Governance system makes their previous contribution less relevant and who might not be entirely happy about switching to a role that focuses more exclusively on governing? You may lose some, but you may be able to keep others if you can show them how their particular skills and talents can still be useful without undermining the board's governing commitment.

Using Existing Board Members' Specific Talents   Board members with suitable skills and talents can be used by your CGO, board committees, or your CEO, assuming they wish to delegate parts of their responsibilities. Tool 8.1 provides some specific ideas on how the talents of board members can be used without interfering with the clarity of delegation from the board to others. It is essential that everyone understands that the accountability of board members who take on these roles is through either the CGO or the board committee or the CEO rather than directly to the board. Otherwise the board will have undermined the authority and accountability of these other delegates and thus its control.

It is also essential that everyone understands that governing volunteer and operational volunteer are two separate roles that should never overlap or otherwise be confounded. If there is any risk of confusion, the operational volunteer role is the one to sacrifice unless the board member resigns. Furthermore, it is vital that the board member offering his or her service as an operational volunteer avoids even the slightest hint of pulling rank or exercising any more influence than a nonboard member operational volunteer and understands that the CEO is totally in charge of whether and how to use such dual service board members and is never to be questioned on the matter by the board (Carver, personal communication, 2008).

What to Do with Board Committees and Officers   The simple rule once you are a Policy Governance board is that board committees and officers need to be confined to roles that assist the board with board work rather than staff with staff work. This does not mean that the people concerned cannot also be helpful in other capacities, but they must do so as individuals, not in a board capacity.

A good way to start is with a blank slate: create any committees or officers you choose to suit your new mode of operation. In terms of committees, you might choose to have an audit committee and a board recruitment or nominations committee. For officers, you might choose to have a board secretary and a vice CGO, but make their conduct part of your CGO's accountability.

The roles of other committees or officers that existed before your adoption of Policy Governance should not be perpetuated without careful examination. For example, finance committees, executive committees, and treasurers are all problematic in that they confuse, and therefore break, the owner-board-CEO chain of accountability. How can the board hold the CEO accountable for the accomplishment of Ends if he or she does not, within board policy, have clear authority over the organization's finances? How can the board provide proper accountability to owners if it has substituted its authority with that of an executive committee? For every committee or officer position you create, you need to be clear about where that position sits in the owner-board-CEO chain of accountability and recognize that there is no such thing as partial accountability.

Recruiting New Board Members It is a good idea for a board embarking on Policy Governance to ready itself for future board recruitment, beginning with the design of the board member job description and invitation. The invitation should come from the board's CGO rather than the CEO because the board will want to establish from the beginning that board membership is a governing rather than managing or advisory job. Even if your board members are appointed by an external authority, there is every reason to seek to influence the process to make sure that your board ends up with suitable candidates. At the end of this chapter, you will find a sample invitation letter for potential board members (see Tool 8.2) and a sample job description for board members (see Tool 8.3).

Your CEO and Staff

The Policy Governance system is designed to ensure that board, CGO, and CEO each know exactly what is required of them and can get on with fulfilling their roles with a minimum of interference. In particular, governing for velocity requires that your CEO be empowered. The good news is that CEO empowerment brings with it not only the possibility of the optimum rate of progress toward your Ends but also the advantages of increased employee contribution, increased work satisfaction, and less conflict. The bad news is that there are clearly risks involved, too. Your CEO might abuse the newly awarded power, exercise it incompetently, or be unwilling to take it on.

A word about risk: In the Policy Governance system, all of this risk is dealt with through regular and rigorous monitoring of compliance with the board's policies as described in Chapter Seven. Indeed, one of the main differences between the Policy Governance approach and other approaches is that *all* of the board's expectations are pre-stated and therefore the criteria for monitoring compliance and competence are clear. Given the fact that the board also has the right to monitor any policy at any time, this clarity provides Policy Governance boards with a much greater than normal level of systematic protection against malfeasance and incompetence. This statement is not to pretend that using Policy Governance is an ironclad guarantee; ultimately, no human construct can provide guarantees. However, it is to say that because using Policy Governance involves comprehensive and systematic review of organizational performance and conformance with board policy, any board that is using it fully should feel a measure of confidence way beyond that felt by other boards. If you are concerned about areas of risk that might be associated with Policy Governance, consult Tool 8.4 at the end of this chapter, which provides strategies to minimize risk.

Strange but true, using Policy Governance, like riding a bike, gives you a mechanism for balancing freedom and control—something we need today more urgently than ever, as the following quote suggests:

> Ultimately, . . . perhaps the greatest danger of the Enron debacle is our possible overreaction—and consequent over-regulation. It's human nature to overreact to dramatic events, like air crashes or, in this case, a landmark bankruptcy. Enron does not, however, represent a systemic problem; the existence of fraud and bad judgment should not, in and of itself, be a basis to change the legal, financial, and accounting infrastructure of business that has—Enron aside—served us so well. Excessive safeguards can stifle business innovation. To remain competitive in a global economy, we must favor flexibility over rigidity, innovation over consistency—even at the risk of another Enron [Schwarcz, 2002, p. 10].

Coping with New Roles   In the same way that boards embarking on Policy Governance should be prepared for the possibility of losing board members who are not willing or able to reinterpret their role, they should be prepared for the eventuality that their current CEO will prove unwilling or unable to cope with the reinterpretation of his or her role. For most CEOs, Policy Governance is a welcome liberation, offering clarity of roles and expectations as well as the opportunity to be fully accountable for the results of their organizational leadership. But for some CEOs, Policy Governance comes as an unwelcome surprise.

For example, a CEO who is used to being the key vision maker may not appreciate the board stepping up their leadership through setting Ends. A CEO who sees the board as a high-level fundraising department may not appreciate the board's concentration on governing rather than helping. And a CEO who is fearful of being held accountable may see the newfound freedom as an invitation to hang himself or herself. This last reaction may be a sign that your CEO is not up to the job, but there could be another reason. Boards often worry about whether they trust their CEO. Policy Governance can expose the fact that your CEO is worried about trusting you.

If the CEO appears uncomfortable with a potential move to Policy Governance, give him or her plenty of opportunity to discuss any worries about it with you and with CEOs of other boards that use the Policy Governance system. However, it is important to be clear that all executive authority comes from the board and that you exist to do the bidding of your owners, not of the CEO. This means that the board should make up its mind itself, with input from its CEO, rather than attempt to make its choice of a new governing system a joint decision.

When a New CEO Is Needed The CEO is usually the board's only direct employee, and the importance of the board's choice of the person to play that role cannot be underestimated. As referred to above, adopting the Policy Governance system is likely to surface any underlying problems relating to a current CEO's competence, use of power, or willingness to be accountable. Unfortunately, the Policy Governance system does not rescue the board from the need to deal with those problems—a topic that is discussed in more detail under CEO evaluation on pages 155–156 in Chapter Seven.

In any case, the board always needs to be prepared for the eventuality that it may need to recruit a new CEO for whatever reason and for ensuring that that person is someone who can do the job. An important way to begin the recruitment process is to prepare a job description of the CEO's role in an organization that practices Policy Governance. Tool 8.5 has a sample job description for a CEO.

ADDRESSING YOUR ORGANIZATION'S CURRENT CIRCUMSTANCES

Embarking on Policy Governance involves considering your organization's current circumstances as well as its people. If your organization is in the middle of a crisis, your board needs to think seriously about how it can find the time and focus necessary to install Policy Governance. If your board foresees needing external help, it needs to consider whether it has the necessary resources to secure that help.

Your board also needs to consider the wider framework in which it operates. Governing for velocity means, in part, having all your documentation aligned. Because laws, regulations, and founding documents, including bylaws, take precedence over your board's policies, your board needs to ensure that those regulations or founding policies do not contain requirements that would prevent the board from agreeing on the policies it wants to have. In particular, your board may find itself in a quandary if laws, regulations, or bylaws appear to require your board to manage the organization directly rather than through your CEO. But remember that although regulations cannot be readily changed, they can be and, indeed, often need to be interpreted.

For example, the statutes of one U.S. state say that the governing boards of college districts shall, among many, many other things, exclude certain books as textbooks; appoint vice chancellors, vice presidents, deans, professors, instructors, lecturers, fellows, and "such other officers and employees as it deems necessary"; and require certain students to sign an affidavit at the time of course registration that the student's vehicle meets the state's standards. Clearly, these boards' jobs would be impossible without considerable delegation, and the boards concerned have no choice but to assume that they can delegate these and other duties to their CEO within requisite governing policies. A "required approvals" agenda can be used to demonstrate your board's direct accountability to external authorities without undoing your ability to hold your CEO accountable. A required approval agenda is a section of the normal agenda that contains items delegated to the CEO within regularly monitored board policy but that the board is compelled to approve by relevant law or contract. Each item on this part of the agenda should cite the relevant law or contract and the relevant monitoring data from the CEO. These approvals can then be moved as one item unless the board agrees to remove them from this part of the agenda. Such agreement should be given only when the board believes that the monitoring data may not be sufficient to demonstrate compliance with relevant board policy.

One of the first things to look at in your bylaws is the very last section, which is usually the section that deals with how they can be amended. Sometimes the board itself can change bylaws, but your board may find that it needs an annual meeting of all the legal members to ratify the board's decision or that it needs the agreement of another body such as a government ministry. If your board decides to seek changes to your organization's bylaws and the changes require the approval of people beyond the board itself, the board will need to consider how likely those people are to agree to any changes the board may wish to make and what kind of education effort may be needed to secure their agreement. Rather than changing your organization's bylaws, your board may simply be able to further interpret them in board policies, but it must be careful that it can justify its policies as a reasonable interpretation rather than a breach of the bylaws. If your board is in doubt, getting legal advice is an essential precaution. Resource B in *Boards That Make a Difference* (Carver, 2006) and Chapter Nine of *Reinventing Your Board* (Carver and Carver, 2006) contain recommendations on bylaws from a Policy Governance perspective.

A number of other circumstances may affect your board as it implements Policy Governance. You will find a summary of some of these circumstances and their implications in Tool 8.6 at the end of this chapter.

PLANNING AND IMPLEMENTING POLICY GOVERNANCE

The third thing that your board needs to consider as it embarks on Policy Governance is its plan for installing and maintaining the system. Any kind of change is likely to cause temporary reductions in performance as people absorb and adjust to the change. Therefore, it is important to plan for sufficient time and resources to fully introduce the change and get your organization past the initial wobbles and on to the high level of performance that your board is seeking.

Plan and Time Frame

An example of a Policy Governance implementation plan, including a time frame, are shown in Tool 8.7 at the end of this chapter. You will need to read the rest of this chapter to understand it fully. This sample plan is based on what is probably the tightest possible schedule for most boards; your board may need to spread the meetings over a considerably longer period while bearing in mind that keeping things as tight as possible will help everyone carry their learning forward from exploration to decision and then to the various stages of the implementation process.

Defining Agreement

Because your board's policies will form an integrated, comprehensive governing system, it makes sense for the board to vote to implement them all at once rather than one by one. This planning stage is a good time for the board to agree on what will represent sufficient agreement when it comes time to adopt its policies. Certainly, the board can change its mind at any time and abandon Policy Governance, but assuming that that is unlikely, the board is committing not only current board members but also all future board members to using these policies. Some boards decide that unanimity is required. Others are unwilling to put themselves in a position whereby just one member could block the decision but seek some measure of consensus. Your board will need to define what it means by *consensus,* for there are many possible interpretations.

Agreeing on Board Policies

Boards usually agree on the set of policies with which they are going to embark on Policy Governance by stepping through a set of drafts that have been constructed in accordance with the special architecture of Policy Governance policies—adding to them, deleting from them, or otherwise amending them to their satisfaction. A set of draft policies for nonprofit and public boards can be found in Resource A of *Reinventing Your Board* (Carver and Carver, 2006, p. 233), and a set of draft policies for the boards of corporations can be found in *Corporate Boards That Create Value* (Carver and Oliver, 2002, pps. 141–175). Policy Governance consultants who have completed the training available through the Policy Governance Academy[SM] can also provide sets of templates and support your board in tailoring them to your organization.

There are a few things to notice before starting on the journey toward implementation of Policy Governance. The first is that the final decision to adopt the new policies does not happen until the very last stage in the process, so people have plenty of time for reconsideration. Your board may also find it helpful to remember that no policy is ever final and that any policy will be open to review at any time after adoption of the board's policy manual, in accordance with whatever process the board has agreed on.

The second thing to notice is the order in which it is suggested that your board might tackle the four policy sections. While there is no hard and fast rule about it, the suggestion that boards defer work on their Ends policies until a separate session after the means sections have been dealt with is based on the assumption that boards might want to consider these expressions of organizational purpose in a different way from the other policies and thus might require more time for discussion and reflection when creating Ends policies. However, if your board feels ready to go to Ends now or even feels that it is essential to do so, that is fine too.

In any case, it is vital for your board to start from clear agreement on who your ownership is (for more on the importance of owners, see Chapter Three) because every single one of your policies should be coming from their perspective, albeit filtered through the board's knowledge and experience. Starting with Governance Process policy means that your board will automatically have agreed on this issue, for the very first policy in that section delineates the board's accountability, but there is no harm in getting a good understanding of ownership first and inserting that decision into your Governance Process policies whenever you actually get to them.

Going through policy drafts requires a lot of concentration and patience. Taking turns at reading the policies aloud can help keep everyone involved. A good idea for helping board members get into the swing is to agree on a set of ground rules for the discussion ahead. Table 8.1 lists the ground rules that were created by the board of a professional association as they embarked on a two-day policy development workshop. The "parking lot" referred to in the list is a device for deferring issues for later consideration. *Later consideration* can mean that the issue gets dealt with at the end of the initial policy deliberation process or whenever the board chooses.

Board members' reaction to the suggestion that they might need to spend a substantial amount of time on policy development can produce some challenges. Some board members will be ready to agree to pretty much everything before they start because they regard the new policies as no more meaningful than the ones that the board had before. Others will want to examine every word out of fear that they are leaving huge holes through which the CEO will be able to drive. The case of the overly agreeable board member is a real problem, for it indicates an avoidance of the power of Policy Governance that may well come back to haunt the board when it is revealed that the board member concerned

> ## Table 8.1
> ## Ground Rules for Initial Policy Development Session
>
> Be brief
>
> Don't repeat
>
> Details, *not* minutiae
>
> Listen to other people
>
> Don't interrupt
>
> No personalities
>
> Operate in the interests of the whole ownership
>
> Respect—no derision
>
> Safe atmosphere
>
> Ask questions
>
> Speak up at the table—not afterward!
>
> Break every hour for five minutes
>
> Add value
>
> Silence = assent
>
> If three or more disagree, reopen discussion for three minutes, then vote or place the issue in the parking lot

has no real commitment to using the system. The overly cautious board member presents a learning opportunity; by asking other board members to help identify the relevant safeguards within the draft policies, such a person will soon find that the policies are indeed comprehensive. A detailed methodology for ensuring that the board's concerns are comprehensively covered in your Executive Limitations policies is described on page 127 in Chapter Six.

Chapters Five and Six of this book offer suggestions that will help your board to develop and maintain its policies in every quadrant—Ends, Executive Limitations, Governance Process, and Board-Management Delegation.

Securing Your Future

Experience shows that if you don't use something, you usually lose it. While you never forget how to ride a bike, the fitness you need to ride it and the bike itself will deteriorate if you don't use it. Similarly, while your policies may remain theoretically in place, if you don't use them, you will lose your ability to govern with velocity and the policies themselves will deteriorate. So, the decision to adopt your policies must also involve deciding how your board is going to keep up the motivation, knowledge, and skills that it needs to keep pedaling forward and avoid unnecessary braking.

Annual Governance Plan and Budget Having an annual governance plan—and an annual governance budget to go with it—are essential for your board's future success. Unless your board members actually experience for themselves the real benefits of governing with velocity, all the hard work and enthusiasm that brought you to this point will have been wasted. Tool 8.8, at the end of this chapter, shows how to create a calendar for annual planning and provides a checklist of items to include.

Notice that your overall plan needs to include subsidiary plans for all aspects of the board's job description. Thus, Tool 8.8 is in fact a composite of plans for ownership linkage, policy development, and monitoring and evaluation, as well as a plan to ensure that the board has all the education it needs to do all this well, including refresher education on using the Policy Governance system.

Policy Reviews While many policies will automatically get reviewed in the course of your board's usual work, it makes sense to set aside time to have a deliberate review of every policy every so often. Some boards do this once a year, examining all the policies in the four main containers in one meeting or across four meetings. Some do it every two years. Others add policy reviews to their monitoring process, inviting board members to consider the policy concerned and raise any issues they think the board should consider on its discussion (as opposed to monitoring) agenda.

To frame a policy review discussion, you might invite individual board members who have a particular interest in certain policies to lead the board in preparing for and conducting the review. Individual board member expertise can be extremely useful when used to bring the whole board up to speed rather than to substitute for full board decision making.

For every policy, the key question to ask is, "Are we still happy with the range of interpretation our policies allow?" To get that the answer, you could ask questions such as these:

- Under what circumstances might this policy, taken in context with all other related policies, be used by the person who has the authority to make any reasonable interpretation of it?

- Would we be happy with how that person could use this policy in those circumstances?

Of course, if new policies were made every time a concern was raised, your carefully constructed policy framework would quickly become unmanageable and therefore meaningless from the viewpoint of accountability. It is essential that any concerns arising from your policy reviews are filtered through the process set out in the section on handling concerns that follows a bit later in this chapter.

Individual Board Meeting Agendas   Once your board's annual plan is in place, building agendas for individual board meetings becomes a significantly easier task because the annual plan gives the CGO and support staff a pre-established framework for every meeting that can be easily completed with any additional input. Tool 8.9 at the end of the chapter is a meeting agenda outline that reflects the annual planning calendar in Tool 8.8. Notice that the core of both is the board's three-part job description of being the link with owners, creating policy that reflects owners' best interests, and assuring performance against that policy.

Your board may want to stick to having a similar agenda for all meetings, as shown in the agenda in Tool 8.9, with an occasional retreat for Ends reviews or other substantive discussions. Or you may want to move toward having fewer, shorter "business meetings" interspersed with longer "discussion meetings" devoted to education and inquiry. Whatever pattern you choose, if your agenda planning is sufficient to have your board truly governing for velocity, your board should experience the following:

- Agendas are driven by governance rather than management.
- Agendas typically focus more on external than internal matters.
- The core of each agenda is planned well in advance through discussion of the board's annual calendar.
- Every item is related to board policy, and therefore the board knows
  - Why it is discussing the matter
  - What it has already said about it
  - What it needs to determine at present
- Because the decision to be made is clear, the information needed to make it is also clear.

- Meetings are focused, and time is used efficiently.
- There is space on every agenda for substantive and free discussion on important issues. The board recognizes the need to reflect individually and together without necessarily having to make a decision.
- Relationships are freed up because everyone's roles are clear.
- The board feels it is engaged with profoundly important and exciting matters.

Once your board has adopted Policy Governance, if any one of the points in the preceding list is not true, board members will know that they have lost their way. In particular, if the board finds that it is getting bogged down with the mechanics of Policy Governance, something is definitely wrong. Remember that Policy Governance is a tool for precision engineering your governance process so that your board is free to focus on creating the future your owners want. You should certainly expect to have to pay attention to your tool in order to keep it sharp, but if you find that the tool, rather than the future, is dominating the agenda, the board is almost certainly using it incorrectly and needs to get some expert help. I explain more about how to get help in the next section.

Board Support Deciding what sort of support you are going to get from where is an essential part of planning for sustainable success with the Policy Governance system. Start with a realistic assessment of what your board will need to help it stay on track, what board members can reasonably expect from themselves and from staff, and what help the board needs to bring in. Whether your board looks for help internally or externally or both, it is critically important that that help be sufficiently skilled and experienced to provide strong and accurate Policy Governance leadership. A good start would be to look at the qualifications that consultants typically list on their Web site or to inquire through the International Policy Governance Association, which maintains a list of full members who are all persons who have taken the highest level of training currently available as well as engaged in continuing education.

Your board also needs to consider cost. How much is effective governance worth to your organization? Just because boards have traditionally spent little or nothing on themselves does not mean that that's the way it should be. Prudence can mean spending more, not less, when it comes to the maintenance of something as critical to your organization's health as its governance. Fees for consulting help range enormously and are sometimes negotiable. Asking other boards that are using Policy Governance is probably one of the best ways to find someone who can work for your board.

Voting to Adopt Your Policies

And now, to the moment of truth in your board's implementation plan—the moment when your board will say good-bye to its previous way of life and start governing for velocity, using its policies to power your organization forward. If everyone on the board is happy to do so, then the board can move ahead, but what happens if one or more board members are not happy?

Making Compromises

It is a natural and often commendable instinct to want to make compromises in an effort to encourage people to support a change that you want to make. Unfortunately, the decision to be a Policy Governance board does not allow for compromise in several critical respects:

- Either your board governs on behalf of your ownership as a whole, or it doesn't.

- Either your board accepts total accountability for your organization, or it doesn't.

- Either your board governs as one group, or it doesn't.

- Either your board exercises accountability through personal control, or it exercises accountability through policy control.

- Either your board takes responsibility for every word of every policy while it is in force, or it doesn't.

Your board can't phase in Policy Governance, because using the Policy Governance system is like riding a bike: you cannot get the benefit it was designed to give you unless you let go of one kind of control in favor of another. In other words, your board cannot get to the speediest possible realization of owners' wishes if it doesn't let go of *personal* control and assume *policy* control. Trying to exercise personal control and policy control together simply does not work, because as soon as your board exercises personal control without reference to its policy, it has, from the delegate's point of view, rendered the policy meaningless.

Combing through a budget in order to render your personal opinion about its merits is one thing. Assessing a budget's compliance with any reasonable interpretation of your board's predetermined policy expectations in regard to budgeting is an entirely different thing. And personal control is not just about board members exercising *individual* control, either. The board as a whole can also exercise personal control in the sense that it can seek to affect an issue or event directly as opposed to using policy control, which affects that same issue or event permanently and in context with all other issues.

Your board needs to decide and let your CEO know what kind of control it is exercising and then hone its skills to exercise that form of control to the very best of its ability. In making that decision, your board needs to be very clear that having policy control is not the same thing as having policies. Table 8.2 shows the difference. All boards have policies to a greater or lesser degree (sometimes hundreds and hundreds of them). But do they have policy *control*?

Handling Concerns Brought to the Board

A new concern can come to the board from anywhere. Whether it comes from a shareholder, a community member, a staff member, the CEO, or a board member, what matters is that the board handles it through its existing policies, starting with clarifying whether the matter should be taken up by the board or CEO.

Filtering issues through the policy framework is essential, for if it is not used or is improperly used, it will soon cease to work. In the same way that the composition of our water supply needs to be carefully managed and monitored to ensure that we all get clean and pleasant-tasting water, your policy framework

Table 8.2
Having Policies Versus Having Policy Control

Having policies means:	Having policy control means:
Having policies—some standing, some ad hoc, some conflicting	Having a system of standing policies that are consistent with each other and thus provide consistent direction
Having some policies on some things	Having policies that encompass all aspects of the board's total accountability
Not knowing who is responsible for what	Knowing who is responsible for what
Having regular reports	Having regular reports that provide interpretations and data that verify policy compliance

needs to be carefully managed and monitored to ensure that you have a well-governed organization. New elements cannot be added until they have been checked in context with all the existing elements to ensure that the integrity of the whole remains.

The policy filtering process, shown in Tool 8.10, can also save enormous amounts of time. You will find that the vast majority of issues are already satisfactorily handled within your existing framework (including the whole monitoring process) and therefore there is nothing more for you to do. Fortuitously enough, that leaves you more time to focus on the bigger and more difficult issues. Certainly it is much better for your organization if the board is spending most of its time ensuring that everyone's efforts are focused on accomplishing the right thing (through Ends development discussions) rather than worrying about what could go wrong along the way.

Public Concerns   Particularly if you are in the public eye, you are likely to find that many of the issues raised with your board fall well into areas in which your CEO currently has the freedom to make any reasonable interpretation of your higher-level policies. Naturally the person or persons raising the issue with you may be disappointed to learn that the board will not be dealing with that issue but referring it back to staff. And naturally, board members would prefer that whoever is raising the issue is not left with the impression that the board doesn't care about him or her. Your board would be wise to have a protocol set out in its Governance Process policy (perhaps within a policy on the board's code of conduct) that ensures that public concerns brought to board members are dealt with in a manner that is both courteous and respectful of the integrity of board-CEO delegation. Chapter Three also gives advice about the successful handling of such communications.

In the interests of preserving integrity, and therefore the usefulness of your policy framework, and remembering that it approaches everything from the top-most level in each issue container, you will often need to abstract up from an individual public concern to see how the board might or might not want to deal with it. For example, consider a parent who is concerned about the quality of her child's teacher and wants that teacher fired. The first issue to address is which of the four main policy containers this fits into. Clearly this is not an issue about the workings of the board itself but one about the workings of the organization, so it must be an Ends or an Executive Limitations matter.

The Ends of a school are (or should be) about the production of educated students rather than about the employment of teachers. Therefore, this matter fits not into the Ends container but into the Executive Limitations container. This means that if the board is going to say anything about it at all, it would be because it saw the need to prohibit something about it on the grounds of ethics or prudence that it believed would not be automatically ruled out by its higher-level policies.

In any case, at the level the issue is presented by this parent, there is nothing the board can do with it, for it is being presented at the level of a one-off customer issue rather than a generic issue that might be of concern to the ownership as a whole. What might the higher-level issues be? All parents may be unhappy with one or more teachers at some point during their child's schooling. Are there any standards of ethics or prudence that the board feels meet either of the tests on page 129 in Chapter Six and that it should therefore impose regarding the treatment of all parents with any sort of complaint? Are there any standards of ethics or prudence that the board feels meet either of the tests on page 129 and that it should therefore impose regarding the treatment of all teachers who find themselves subject to parental complaints?

Notice that at this level of creating policies to govern the handling of all parents with any sort of complaint, the board might make a real and lasting contribution. And also notice the amount of damage that could be done if the board jumped into making individual event-driven decisions—for example, by firing the teacher. Trying to solve problems individually generally serves only to create more problems. Governing involves creating a logical and coherent framework in which all problems can be solved rather than coming up with individual solutions. As the ultimate leadership within the organization, the board needs to focus on creating the overall context for everything the organization does rather than on reacting to it.

CEO Concerns CEOs may bring issues to your board for several reasons:

- They may believe that they do not have the authority to decide what should be done.

- They may be uncertain if they have the authority to decide what should be done.

- They may not want to be responsible for deciding what should be done.

If your board is using the Policy Governance system, the first two issues listed will become irrelevant; the CEO will be clear where the limits of his or her authority lie because your board will have made them explicit in its policies. Most CEOs relish having clear authority and are happy to accept the increased accountability that comes with it. Nevertheless, in some cases, your CEO may continue to bring you issues that he or she should be dealing with. The board must remain firm. If you do the CEO's job for the CEO, you effectively don't have a CEO. This is not to say that the CEO cannot ask board members for advice. However, it is to say that the board needs to be completely clear that this is the CEO's decision, not theirs. Whether the board's advice, or anyone else's, is sought and whether that advice turns out to be good or bad, the board will still regard the CEO as fully accountable for the result.

Temporary Concerns Circumstances may arise that cause you to want to alter your policy temporarily. For example, if your organization embarks on a major building project, you might wish to prohibit particular choices on grounds of ethics or prudence that could come up in relation to that project. This is fine, but to avoid unnecessary future clutter, the policy needs a relevant expiration date on it and the board calendar must have regular monitoring and a final review of it before that date.

Handling Everyday Board-CEO Communications

Using the Policy Governance system means that the board and CEO have clear roles within distinct domains, all guided by a transparent set of policies. This does not mean that interaction between the board and CEO becomes either unnecessary or undesirable. As seen on pages 131–132 in Chapter Six, one of the Executive Limitations policy templates, Communication and Support to the Board, in fact sets out some of the policies that you might wish to create in order to ensure that the communication you desire takes place in terms of ensuring that you get the support and information you feel you need.

You need monitoring reports from your CEO as set out in your Board-Management Delegation policy, but you will probably also want to ensure that the CEO keeps you up to date with current events, and particularly any events that could put the organization in jeopardy. You may also want to hear from the CEO about what the staff have to say on various issues. You may well also want the CEO's practical assistance with board tasks such as ownership linkage and circulation of board documentation. All of this, and indeed all board-CEO interaction, is fine as long as the CEO is held accountable for acting in accordance with any reasonable interpretation of board policy.

Practice, Practice, Practice

Daniel T. Willingham, associate professor of cognitive psychology and neuroscience at the University of Virginia and author of *Cognition: The Thinking Animal,* observes that in order for you to really master something, it has to become part of you. He reports, "The unexpected finding from cognitive science is that practice *does not* make perfect. Practice until you are perfect and you will be perfect only briefly. What's necessary is sustained practice" (Willingham, 2004). Also highlighting the need for lots of practice, Joel A. Barker points out that when a paradigm shifts, everyone goes back to zero and that this is particularly hard for those who were most expert and successful in the preceding paradigm (Barker, 1992).

What these two points mean for Policy Governance boards is that they need to underpin the effective use of policy control with continual training and practice. Policy Governance is more than a set of policies; it is a specific kind of practice that requires discipline and commitment. It may feel uncomfortable at first, but over time, it will feel more and more natural—just like riding a bike.

MOVING ON

My favorite quotation about leadership, which applies powerfully to boards, is, "Leadership is about making shared meaning out of complexity" (Horth and Palus, 2002).

Organizations are complex entities operating in an increasingly complex world. As the highest authority within organizations, boards are responsible for creating shared sense out all of that complexity between owners, board members, and staff. I hope this book has helped you understand Policy Governance as a system for doing just that: for creating a powerful context of values governing everything that your organization is and does and a way to be accountable for making those values count.

With a well-justified decision to move to Policy Governance and with its policies, including a maintenance plan, in place, your board is ready to start governing for velocity. The training wheels are off, and your board and your organization should be surging forward. The earlier parts of this book provide much information that you may wish to return to occasionally in order to deepen your understanding of your new policy controls as you put them into practice. Happy pedaling!

TOOLS

TOOL 8.1 USING POLICY GOVERNANCE BOARD MEMBERS' INDIVIDUAL TALENTS

Individual board members' skills and talents can be very helpful to organizations. On Policy Governance boards, however, it is essential that their use does not interfere with the clarity of the board's delegation to others. Here are some examples of roles that an individual board member can usefully play. They are divided between roles in which the board member would be accountable to the CGO or relevant board committee, because they would have been delegated by the CGO or relevant board committee, and roles in which the board member would be accountable to the CEO, because they would have been delegated by the CEO.

Roles in Which Accountability Is to the CGO or Relevant Board Committee

- *Research and education for policy development:* Equipping the full board with the research and education necessary to develop board policy

- *Education for policy monitoring:* Equipping the full board with the education necessary to monitor board policy in a particular area of expertise

- *Coordination of the board's education:* Ensuring that the board implements a plan for board education, including orientation of new board members

- *Coordination of ownership linkage:* Ensuring that the board implements a plan for communicating with owners

- *Coordination of the board's calendar:* Ensuring that the board has an up-to-date annual calendar and acts in accordance with it
- *Assistance with optional board jobs:* Accomplishing specific results in any areas of accountability that the board may have reserved for itself, such as fundraising or public policy development—for example,
  - Raising a specified amount of money
  - Forming an advisory committee, including persons with specified experience relating to the board's (rather than the CEO's) work
  - Developing or communicating the board's public policy positions in an area of expertise

Roles in Which Accountability Is to the CEO or Other Staff Member

At the CEO's request, board members can advise or assist the CEO or other members of staff or staff committees with anything that they mutually agree on.

TOOL 8.2   SAMPLE INVITATION LETTER TO A PROSPECTIVE POLICY GOVERNANCE BOARD MEMBER

Dear xxx,

You have been recommended to our board as someone who could be a very valuable addition to our governing team, and I am therefore writing to invite you to put your name forward.

We govern [*name of organization*] on behalf of [*ownership*] and aim to reflect their collective best interests in all our decision making. We believe that it is our role to create the future and to ensure the organization's performance against our specific requirements in terms of strategic outcomes and ethical and prudential limitations.

I attach a job description; information about our organization; profiles of our current board members; our board policies, including our board member code of conduct; and a description of the process for selecting and orienting new board members.

We very much hope that you will consider joining our leadership group. A member of our Board Development Committee has been asked to contact you by phone to answer any questions you may have about this invitation and to discuss it with you. If you have any questions in the meantime, please do not hesitate to contact me at 555–5555.

Yours sincerely,

xxxxxxxxxxxx,
Chief Governance Officer, xxx Board of Directors

TOOL 8.3 JOB DESCRIPTION FOR A POLICY GOVERNANCE BOARD MEMBER

The Board's Role

The board of xxx acts as the representative of the organization's legal and moral ownership to ensure that xxx makes a valuable difference for its beneficiaries in an ethical and prudent manner. As such, the board has three main tasks:

1. Being accountable to the organization's owners for the organization's direction and performance

2. Producing written governing policies that provide comprehensive direction and control

3. Ensuring the organization's performance against the board's governing policies

The current board consists of _____ members who each serve a _____ -year term. Meetings are held _____. The annual meeting is held in _____ and our annual retreat is usually held in _____.

Your Role

In order to ensure that the diversity of our ownership is reflected as fully as possible in our work, we govern as a full team. We occasionally use committees to research issues or undertake specific tasks for us, but they are never used to substitute for the full board's authority.

Your role is to contribute to the work of the team (see "The Board's Role") as fully as possible. Thus, your work involves

- Seeking to reflect the wishes of the ownership as a whole
- Defining the organization's future direction
- Defining the organization's values in regard to ethics and prudence
- Monitoring organizational and board performance

Your Contribution

Your contribution is expected to take the form of

- Being part of our collective effort to link with our ownership
- Helping to determine, collect, and analyze decision and monitoring information
- Participating assertively in deliberation at board meetings
- Abiding by established policies

Your Qualities

We are looking for people who

- Are committed to our organization's area of concern
- Tend to think in terms of systems and context
- Enjoy dealing with values, vision, and the long term
- Are willing to share power in group process
- Are willing to delegate substantial amounts of decision making to others

For More Information

About the Recruitment Process

[Description of recruitment process and timelines]
Please contact *[Name of person responsible]*

About Our Board Process

Our board uses Policy Governance® as developed by John Carver. The authoritative Web site can be accessed at www.policygovernance.com

and further information is available through www.policygovernanceas sociation.org.

Our code of conduct is attached, and our full set of policies can be seen on our Web site at www.organization.org.

About Our Organization

[Description of your organization]

TOOL 8.4 RISKS AND MITIGATING STRATEGIES IN THE APPLICATION OF POLICY GOVERNANCE

All agreed-on strategies should be put into the board's policy and therefore become subject to regular monitoring and evaluation.

RISK	MITIGATING STRATEGIES
A. Board's policies are inadequate.	Occasionally review the robustness of board policies with appropriate specialist input (for example, financial and legal).
B. Delegates fail to operate according to policies.	1. Regularly monitor every policy. 2. Require disclosure of interpretations and data. 3. Impose appropriate consequences for noncompliance. 4. Ensure that the board has clearly stated its right to subject any policy to direct board inspection or external audit at any time.
C. Monitoring reports are insufficient for the board to know whether delegate is operating according to policies.	1. Refuse to accept insufficient monitoring reports; i.e., treat as a failure to demonstrate compliance. 2. Require resubmission of reports within a specified time frame. 3. Inform CEO about education and training resources for producing monitoring reports.

RISK	MITIGATING STRATEGIES
D. Board finds out about a failure too late.	1. Oblige delegate (through Executive Limitations policy) to inform the board in a timely manner of any actual or anticipated noncompliance with any policy.
	2. Monitor policies the board regards as particularly critical with appropriate frequency.
	3. Purchase liability insurance for board members.
	4. Ensure that the board has a clear policy statement that sets out its right to subject any policy to direct board inspection or external audit at any time.
E. Board is inadequately rigorous in monitoring its policies.	1. Ensure that board members receive education and training on how to monitor policies.
	2. Ask board members to consider the kinds of things that could be going wrong and their responsibility to ensure they are going right.
	3. Remind CGO and all board members of their obligation to call the board to account as needed.
	4. Use external monitoring for a larger number of policies.
F. Board fails to respond appropriately to noncompliance.	1. Ensure that the board receives specific education and training on how to handle noncompliance.
	2. Ask board members to consider their obligation to their owners and require CGO to call board to account.
G. The delegate deliberately attempts to mislead the board.	See B and D.

TOOL 8.5 SAMPLE CEO JOB DESCRIPTION FROM A POLICY GOVERNANCE BOARD

The board of xxx is currently seeking a chief executive officer to lead the organization toward the accomplishment of an ambitious set of strategic outcomes (Ends) for *[specify beneficiaries]*.

Your Qualities

You will have considerable freedom to accomplish the board's Ends within clearly stated limitations related to prudence and ethics. To be a successful candidate, you will need to be able to demonstrate:

- A clear grasp of and commitment to the board's Ends.
- An appreciation of the challenges you are likely to face in fulfilling those Ends
- The ability to develop effective strategies within a rapidly changing environment
- High-level management skills
- The highest standards of personal integrity
- Strong commitment to the value of accountability

Your Role

Your role will be to lead the staff of the organization and be accountable for all they do in pursuit of the board's Ends. Thus, your work will involve

- Being the link between the board and the operating organization
- Ensuring that the organization is operating within a reasonable interpretation of the board's Ends and Limitations policies
- Keeping the board informed of anticipated or actual noncompliance with any board policy
- Providing the board with the decision information it requires to keep its policies current
- Providing monitoring information, including policy interpretations and data, according to the board's monitoring schedule

For More Information

About Our Organization

[Description of your organization]

About the Recruitment Process

[Description of recruitment process and timelines]
Please contact [Name of person responsible]

About the Terms and Conditions of Employment

[Description of terms and conditions]

About Our Board's Policies

Our board uses the Policy Governance® system as developed by John Carver. The authoritative Web site can be found at www.policygovernance.com. Further information is available through www.policygovernanceassociation.org. A full set of our current policies is available from xxxxxx.

TOOL 8.6   SPECIAL CIRCUMSTANCES AND THEIR IMPLICATIONS FOR POLICY GOVERNANCE BOARDS

CIRCUMSTANCE	STRATEGIES FOR POLICY GOVERNANCE BOARD
Spiritual organization	In Governance Process policy, distinguish between accountability to spiritual leadership for upholding the integrity of "the word" and accountability to the lay community for governing the operational organization that spreads the "the word."
Judicial: The organization is responsible for the conduct of judicial or quasi-judicial hearings.	If the board is going to govern and directly produce "fair hearings," add this term to the board's job description in Governance Process policy. If the board is going to hold the CEO accountable for fair hearings, address that in Ends and Executive Limitations policies.

CIRCUMSTANCE	STRATEGIES FOR POLICY GOVERNANCE BOARD
Federation	If there is a central office, distinguish whether it is "owned" by the local offices or vice versa. Does the central office exist to provide secretariat or leadership to the local offices? If the latter, how does leadership get provided? Reflect the answers in relevant policies.
Subsidiarity: Another authority hires and fires the organization's CEO.	Acknowledge the reality in your Governance Process policies but also state that your board will hold itself to a standard of accountability to your owners as if it had the authority to hire and fire the CEO.
Sole shareholder	Acknowledge the reality in your Governance Process policies. Recognize a wider moral ownership if your board believes that conducting itself accordingly would be in your sole shareholder's best interests.
Executives on the board: The CEO or other executives from the organization are on the board.	In your Governance Process policy on board members' conduct, ensure that executives from the organization do not vote on any matter on which they have a conflict of interest.
There are no staff.	Set expectations in board policy, assigning responsibilities either to a volunteer CEO or to a volunteer management committee that operates separately from the board (even if its membership is coterminous). Monitor performance against your policies.
Advisory group	An advisory group has no accountability and therefore no need for Policy Governance.
Two CEOs	Either treat both as one CEO for accountability purposes, or attempt to divide accountability in Ends policies, recognizing that this means that the board has not delegated responsibility for the fulfillment of its broadest End.
Regulatory: The organization is responsible for regulating a community or profession.	In Governance Process policy, include "a well-regulated community" (or profession) in the board's job description.
Treasurer elected at large	In Governance Process policy, specify that person's role in regard to auditing of the monitoring reports received by the board.

CIRCUMSTANCE	STRATEGIES FOR POLICY GOVERNANCE BOARD
CGO or CEO elected at large	Discuss with legal ownership with a view to either changing the relevant bylaw or creating a Governance Process policy that specifies that person's role be consistent with use of Policy Governance system.
Fund management: The organization is responsible for safekeeping or investment of funds that belong to others.	Where this is a significant purpose of the organization, delegate to CEO within appropriate Ends and Limitations. Where this is a small and distinct responsibility and the board has the capacity, consider retaining "a prudently managed xxx fund" (or some such language) as a board job product.
Holding company	Use Governance Process policies to clarify the relationship between the board of the holding company and the board of the subsidiary company. Is the subsidiary company board directly accountable to the holding company board within Ends and Executive Limitations set by the holding company board? Or is the subsidiary company board directly accountable to the holding company CEO within Ends and Executive Limitations set by the holding company CEO?

Note: See also Carver (2006).

TOOL 8.7   SAMPLE IMPLEMENTATION PLAN FOR POLICY GOVERNANCE

The following plan assumes that the decision to implement Policy Governance was made before Week 1 but that adoption of policies has not been formally considered.

Week 1

1. Agree on implementation plan and date for Policy Blitz workshop (one month's notice)

Week 5

1. Hold Policy Blitz workshop (usually 1.5 days)

    a. Governance Process

    b. Executive Limitations

    c. Board-Management Delegation

    d. Agree on holding policy for Ends—for example:

    Whatever Ends the board has stated or implied in previous decisions or approvals will stay unchanged, pending formal adoption of Ends policies.

2. Produce first draft of board policy manual, based on work done in Policy Blitz workshop

Weeks 6, 7, and 8

1. Review legal implications of founding documentation (to note or to consult with legal counsel about any conflicts with the draft policies)

    a. Founding legislation or regulations (where applicable)

    b. Letters patent, memorandum of incorporation

    c. Bylaws, articles of incorporation

2. Review implications of previous board policies (to check whether values therein are encompassed by the new policies)

3. Review management implications of draft policies (to offer opportunity for further board-CEO consultation in order to address any staff concerns about the draft policies)

Week 9

1. Hold second board workshop to consider any proposals for policy amendments arising from reviews of implications: legal, previous board policy and management, identified in weeks 6, 7, and 8 (usually half a day)

2. Produce second draft of board policy manual

Week 12

1. Hold formal board vote on new board policy manual

2. Agree on board's annual plan for the forthcoming year, including:

    a. Plan for continuing board support with Policy Governance

    b. Plan for board education for all governing responsibilities

    c. Plan for communication with ownership

    d. Schedule for monitoring reports

        i. CEO performance

        ii. Board performance

    e. Other board dates arising from bylaws or board policy

3. Agree on date for first workshop on Ends development

4. Evaluate Policy Governance implementation plan

Immediately Following Board Policy Adoption

1. CEO begins work to produce monitoring interpretations and data collection

2. Staff training is secured as necessary

TOOL 8.8   ANNUAL PLANNING FOR A POLICY GOVERNANCE BOARD

Create a calendar for the year, with months on one side and categories of board activity across the top. Reference relevant board policies and bylaws.

	Ownership Connection	Policy Decisions— Organization	Policy Decisions— Board	Other[a]
January	Annual meeting		Annual review of Governance Process policies	
February		Reconsideration of Treatment of Staff policy	Annual board budget approved	

	Ownership Connection	Policy Decisions— Organization	Policy Decisions— Board	Other[a]
March	Focus groups for key influencers		Reconsideration of board members' code of conduct	
April	Publication of owners' guide	Annual review of Ends policies	Board succession planning	
and so on . . .				

[a]See the text that follows for other possible headings.

For each month, consider what, if anything, the board will do under the following headings, each of which comes directly from the board's job description.

Ownership Connection

Enter key activities from the board's ownership linkage plan (see Chapter Three). Don't forget to include planning for the annual meeting, the annual report, receipt of the auditor's report, and changes to bylaws.

Policy Decisions—Governing the Organization

Enter any decisions that the board needs to make about Ends or Executive Limitations policies, including any annual policy reviews that are due.

Policy Decisions—Governing the Board

Enter any decisions that the board needs to make about Governance Process or Board-Management Delegation policies, including any annual policy reviews that are due.

Enter any decisions or actions that are needed in regard to board succession planning, annual board planning, annual budgeting for board work, annual disclosure of interests per the board's conflict of interest policy, audit activities, or board officer elections.

Enter any decisions or actions that are needed on matters of CEO employment, compensation, or succession planning.

Monitoring and Evaluation—Organization

Enter the dates that monitoring reports are due from the CEO on Ends and Executive Limitations policies. Enter the date of the CEO's annual evaluation.

Monitoring and Evaluation—Board

Enter the dates that monitoring reports are due from the CGO or the board on Governance Process and Board-Management Delegation Policies. Enter the date of the annual board evaluation.

Board Education

Enter key activities from your plan for board education—for example, to inform the following activities:

- Ownership linkage

- Policy development

- Monitoring and evaluation

- New board member orientation

- Any other products for which the board has taken responsibility

TOOL 8.9   SAMPLE AGENDA FOR A BOARD MEETING

Not all items will be relevant to all agendas. Reference relevant board policies and bylaws.

Times are approximate and assume a three-hour meeting.

Call to Order—5 Minutes

1. Welcome—PROCEDURAL

2. Attendance—PROCEDURAL

3. Appointment of Meeting Monitor—PROCEDURAL

4. Declaration of Conflict of Interest—PROCEDURAL

5. Approval of Minutes of Last Meeting—DECISION

6. Adoption of Agenda—DECISION

Required Approvals—5 Minutes

[These are items that have been delegated to the CEO within regularly monitored board policy but that the board is compelled to approve by relevant law or contract. Each item on this part of the agenda cites the relevant law or contract and the relevant monitoring data from the CEO. These approvals will be moved as one item unless removed from this part of the agenda by agreement of the board. Board agreement for removing an item from the required approvals agenda will be given only when the board believes that the monitoring data may not be sufficient to demonstrate compliance with relevant board policy.]

7. Required Approvals—DECISION

Performance Management—20 Minutes

[Consideration of monitoring reports due and received since last meeting]

8. Receipt and Approval of CEO Monitoring Reports—MONITORING

   Due this month: EL 2, 5, & 7. Circulated to board on *[date]*

9. Receipt and Approval of Board Monitoring Reports—MONITORING

   Due this Month: GP 4 & 5, BMD 2. Circulated to board on *[date]*

Ownership Linkage—30 Minutes

10. Ownership Linkage Activities per Board's Annual Plan—DECISION

Board Education—60 Minutes

11. Board Education Presentations and Discussions per Board's Annual Plan—DECISION

Policy Development—25 Minutes

[Assuming one item under 12 and one item under 13 below]

12. Proposed Additions or Amendments to Board Policies—DECISION

   - Governing the Organization
   - Governing the Board

13. Regular Policy Review—DECISION
    - Governing the Organization
    - Governing the Board

Other Board Jobs—15 Minutes

[Assuming one item under 14 and one item under 15 below]

14. Governance Process Matters—DECISION

15. Advocacy or Fundraising—DECISION

Other Information—12 Minutes

[This item may include written or verbal information presented by whomever the CEO chooses.]

16. Communication and Support to the Board—INFORMATION

Closing—8 Minutes

17. Date and Place of Next Meeting—PROCEDURAL

18. Meeting Evaluation—(Meeting Monitor's Report)—PROCEDURAL

19. Close of Meeting—PROCEDURAL

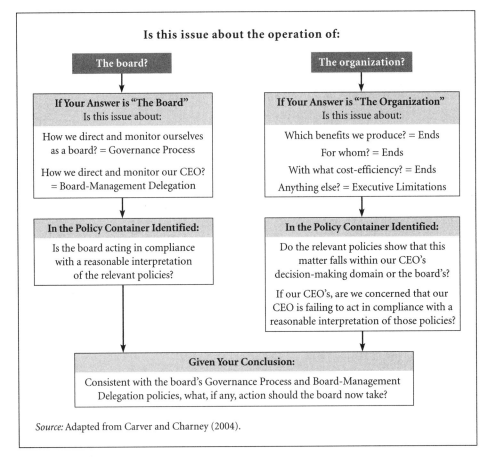

Is this issue about the operation of:

| The board? | The organization? |

If Your Answer is "The Board"
Is this issue about:

How we direct and monitor ourselves as a board? = Governance Process

How we direct and monitor our CEO? = Board-Management Delegation

If Your Answer is "The Organization"
Is this issue about:

Which benefits we produce? = Ends

For whom? = Ends

With what cost-efficiency? = Ends

Anything else? = Executive Limitations

In the Policy Container Identified:

Is the board acting in compliance with a reasonable interpretation of the relevant policies?

In the Policy Container Identified:

Do the relevant policies show that this matter falls within our CEO's decision-making domain or the board's?

If our CEO's, are we concerned that our CEO is failing to act in compliance with a reasonable interpretation of those policies?

Given Your Conclusion:

Consistent with the board's Governance Process and Board-Management Delegation policies, what, if any, action should the board now take?

Source: Adapted from Carver and Charney (2004).

POLICY GOVERNANCE RESOURCES

Many of the original resources about Policy Governance have been updated (in some cases, several times), and the overall list continues to grow. The list here has been categorized to help you identify which resources may be most useful to you given your board's stage of exploration or implementation.

BRIEF INTRODUCTIONS

For Nonprofit Organizations and Government

"Carver's Policy Governance® Model in Nonprofit Organizations" by John Carver and Miriam Carver http://www.carvergovernance.com/pg-np.htm

For Equity Corporations

"A Theory of Corporate Governance: Finding a New Balance for Boards and Their CEOs" by John Carver http://www.carvergovernance.com/pg-corp.htm

FULL INTRODUCTIONS

For Nonprofit Organizations and Government

Carver, John. *Boards That Make a Difference: A New Design for Leadership in Nonprofit and Public Organizations.* (3rd ed.) San Francisco: Jossey-Bass, 2006.

For Equity Corporations

Carver, John, and Caroline Oliver. *Corporate Boards That Create Value: Governing Company Performance from the Boardroom.* San Francisco: Jossey-Bass, 2002. Foreword by Sir Adrian Cadbury.

IMPLEMENTING POLICY GOVERNANCE

Carver, John, and Miriam Carver. *Reinventing Your Board: A Step-by-Step Guide to Implementing Policy Governance.* (2nd ed.) San Francisco: Jossey-Bass, 2006.

SHARPENING THE SAW

Generic

Carver, John. *John Carver on Board Leadership.* San Francisco: Jossey-Bass, 2002. This book brings together selected writings from the creator of Policy Governance, "the world's most provocative and systematic governance model."

Carver, John, and Miriam Carver (eds.). *Board Leadership: Policy Governance in Action.* San Francisco: Jossey-Bass. Strongly recommended for boards that are implementing Policy Governance, this newsletter of eight to twelve pages, edited by John Carver and Miriam Carver, is published six times a year. The Carvers and other Policy Governance consultants provide short, clear articles with a lot of practical detail about using the Policy Governance model. Available from John Wiley & Sons in paper and online versions. http://www. josseybass.com/WileyCDA/WileyTitle/productCd-BL.html.

Carver, Miriam, and Bill Charney. *The Board Member's Playbook: Using Policy Governance to Solve Problems, Make Decisions, and Build a Stronger Board.* San Francisco: Jossey-Bass, 2004. This book enables boards to build and maintain governance skills with carefully crafted exercises (rehearsals), using a simple question-and-answer sequence.

Conduff, Mike, Carol Gabanna, and Catherine Raso. *The OnTarget Board Member: Eight Indisputable Behaviors.* Denton, Tex.: Elim Group Publishing, 2007. This novelette traces a board member's experience of "discovery and accomplishment" in learning board leadership the Policy Governance way. Order from www.ontargetconsulting.com.

Oliver, Caroline (general editor), with Mike Conduff, Susan Edsall, Carol Gabanna, Randee Loucks, Denise Paszkiewicz, Catherine Raso, and Linda Stier. *The Policy Governance Fieldbook: Practical Lessons, Tips, and Tools from the Experiences of Real-World Boards*. San Francisco: Jossey-Bass, 1999. This book reviews the journey toward Policy Governance and offers a collection of practical tools based on case studies from boards that use Policy Governance.

Specific Aspects

Carver, John, and Miriam Mayhew Carver. *CarverGuides*. San Francisco: Jossey-Bass, 1997. These sixteen- to-twenty-five-page booklets are written in a readable style. They are excellent for helping to orient new board members to Policy Governance. CarverGuide titles include

1. Basic Principles of Policy Governance

2. Your Roles and Responsibilities as a Board Member

3. Three Steps to Fiduciary Responsibility

4. The Chairperson's Role as Servant-Leader to the Board

5. Planning Better Board Meetings

6. Creating a Mission That Makes a Difference

7. Board Assessment of the CEO

8. Board Self-Assessment

9. Making Diversity Meaningful in the Boardroom

10. Strategies for Board Leadership

11. Board Members as Fund-Raisers, Advisers, and Lobbyists

12. The CEO Role Under Policy Governance

A new series of these guides will be available from Jossey-Bass by spring 2009. It will be titled the Policy Governance Guide Series on Board Leadership and there will be six instead of twelve guides, all authored by John and Miriam Carver. The individual titles are: *The Policy Governance Model and the Role of the Board Member; Ends and the Ownership; The Governance of Financial Management; Adjacent Leadership Roles: CGO and CEO; Evaluating CEO and Board Performance; Implementing Policy Governance and Staying on Track.*

Jannice Moore and Associates, Ltd. *REALBoard Tool Kit™*. Vol. 1: *Meaningful Monitoring,* 2005. Vol. 2: *Board Self-Evaluation,* 2006. Calgary, Canada: The Governance Coach™. Jannice Moore has drawn on her extensive experience as a Policy Governance consultant to provide a toolkit to assist boards in using the Policy Governance model effectively. Volume 1 addresses questions about the process of monitoring the CEO, including how a board attends to this important task without spending undue time doing so. Volume 2 addresses the process of making board self-evaluation a meaningful and valuable part of the governance process.

SPECIALIZED APPLICATIONS

Ernst & Young, Peter Wallace, and John Zinkin. *Corporate Governance: Mastering Business in Asia.* Singapore: John Wiley & Sons, 2005. This book has a Foreword by John Carver and a description of Policy Governance. The emphasis is on the development of Asian businesses and the shareholders' viewpoint.

Moore, Jannice. *Governance for Health System Trustees.* Ottawa: Canadian Healthcare Association Press, 2004. This book is geared to the needs of health system governors. Based on practical experience in applying the Policy Governance model to the boards of health care organizations, it provides (1) the questions you as a board member need to ask yourself and (2) the answers, so you can determine if you're doing the right things to ensure the long-term future of your health organization.

Royer, Gene. *School Board Leadership 2000: The Things Staff Didn't Tell You at Orientation.* N.p.: Gene Royer, 1996. This book was written by a Texas-based consultant who has worked with Carver's model for a number of years, specifically with school boards. All of the examples are school related. Further information can be found at http://generoyer.com.

AUDIOVISUAL RESOURCES

Carver, John. *Empowering Boards for Leadership: Redefining Excellence in Governance.* San Francisco: Jossey-Bass, 1992. A two-cassette audio program. (Two hours) Draws on John Carver's book *Boards That Make a Difference* to reveal how boards can see past the clutter of day-to-day details to provide real governance for their organizations.

Carver, John, and Miriam Carver. *The Policy Governance Model: An Introduction by John and Miriam Carver.* Coproduced by Miriam Carver and the International Policy Governance Association. 2008. This DVD features John and Miriam Carver explaining the Policy Governance model in five modules. It can be ordered from the International Policy Governance Association. For details, go to www.policygovernanceassociation.org.

Jannice Moore and Associates, Ltd. *REALBoard On-Line Learning.* Calgary, Canada: The Governance Coach™, 2008. This modular course covers the principles of Policy Governance. Each module can be completed in fifteen to twenty minutes, so that you can learn in convenient segments that match your schedule. For more details, go to www.governancecoach.com.

BOARD MANAGEMENT SYSTEMS

OurBoardroom™: Your Policy Governance Partner. OurBoardroom Technologies Inc. OurBoardroom is an online system for taking your governance process to a new level of efficiency, accessibility, and sustainability. Built on the logic of Policy Governance, OurBoardroom helps boards organize and simplify their operations and documentation, including policies, agendas, monitoring reports, and other information in one clear and seamless system. For further details, contact info@ourboardroom.com.

COURSES

Policy Governance® Academy℠. Advanced sessions conducted by Miriam Carver and John Carver in theory and implementation for consultants and organizational leaders. Proof of sufficient Policy Governance understanding for participation is judged by Miriam and John Carver based on a written application. For more information, contact Ivan Benson at ivanbenson@carvergovernance.com or phone 404–728–9444.

Public workshops. Information about public workshops can be found on the Web sites of the Carvers (www.carvergovernance.com) and other Policy Governance consultants (see below) as well as through the International Policy Governance Association (www.policygovernanceassociation.org) and the UK Policy Governance Association (www.ukpga.org.uk).

INDIVIDUAL BOARD CONSULTANCY

The International Policy Governance Association (IPGA) and the UK Policy Governance Association can help you find consultants who have completed the Policy Governance Academy. You can also try a Web search using the term "policy governance" or "Carver governance." Be sure to check that the persons concerned have completed the Academy.

ASSOCIATIONS

International Policy Governance Association (IPGA). This is an independent charitable organization formed in 1999 and incorporated in 2001 in order to create a forum for nurturing responsible governance and effective, ethical governance consulting. The association seeks to have an impact on the understanding, use, and teaching of the Policy Governance system and welcomes into membership boards using Policy Governance, as well as individuals or organizations that use or teach Policy Governance or are interested in supporting IPGA and its purpose. IPGA is incorporated in the state of New York as a 501(c)(3) charitable organization.

U.K. Policy Governance Association (UKPGA). This is a nonprofit company limited by guarantee and governed by a trustee board comprising graduates of the Policy Governance Academy. UKPGA is dedicated to advancing owner-accountable, ethical, and effective governance using the Carver Policy Governance model. Registered in England and Wales as Policy Governance Association (UK) No. 5742306.

RESOURCES IN OTHER LANGUAGES

Dutch

Verantwoord besturen. Jan Maas and Helmie van Ravestein, 2006. The first comprehensive description of the Policy Governance model in Dutch: its theory, methods, and instruments and what it has to offer to Dutch board structures and governance issues. Foreword by John Carver. For information and ordering: www.maasgovernance.com

French

"Leadership Du Conseil D'adminstration: The Policy Governance Model." *Gouvernance—Revue Internationale,* 2000, *2*(1), 100–108.

Portuguese

Conselhos de Administração que Geram Valor: Dirigindo o Desempenho da Empresa a Partir do Conselho. São Paulo: Editora Cultrix. Order at www.pensamento -cultrix.com.brn. Translated from John Carver with Caroline Oliver, *Corporate Boards That Create Value: Governing Company Performance from the Boardroom.* San Francisco: Jossey-Bass, 2002.

Russian

Carver, John. "Model corporativnogo upravleniya: novyi balance mezhdu sovetom directorov i managementom companii". *Economischeski Vestnic,* 2003, no. 9, 101–110. This article was originally published as "Leadership du conseil d'administration: The Policy Governance Model," *Gouvernance—Revue Internationale,* 2000, *2*(1), 100–108. A summary of the article appeared as "Teoriya Corporativnogo Upravleniya: Poisk Novogo Balansa Mezhdu Sovetom Directorov i Generalnym Directorom," by John Carver in E. Spir (ed.), *Russian Enterprises in the Transitive Economy,* Materials of the International Conference, Yaroslavl State University, Vol. 1, Oct. 29–30, 2002, pp. 47–50.

Spanish

"Un modelo de Gobierno Corporativo para el Mexico moderno" (A Corporate Governance Model for a Modern Mexico), *Ejecutivos de Finanzas* (Instituto Mexicano de Ejecutivos de Finanzas). no. 9, 2006, 1–15.

"Una Teoria De Gobierno Corporativo" by the Oficina del la Presidencia para la Innovación Gubernamental, Mexico City, 2001. This article was originally published as "Leadership du conseil d'adminstration: The Policy Governance Model," *Gouvernance—Revue Internationale,* 2000, *2*(1), 100–108.

REFERENCES

Alchian, A., and Demsetz, H. "Production, Information Costs, and Economic Organization." *American Economic Review*, 1972, *62*, 777–795.

Barker, J. A. *Paradigms: The Business of Discovering the Future.* New York: Morrow 1992.

Bullen, P. "Writing Policy and Organisational Manuals." Coogee, NSW, Australia: Management Alternatives, n.d.

Campbell, K. "Legal Rights." Stanford Encyclopaedia of Philosophy. Apr. 15, 2005. http://plato.stanford.edu/entries/legal-rights/.

Carver, J. *Boards That Make a Difference: A New Design for Leadership in Nonprofit and Public Organizations.* (3rd ed.) San Francisco: Jossey-Bass, 2006.

Carver, J., and Carver, M. *Reinventing Your Board: A Step-by-Step Guide to Implementing Policy Governance.* (2nd ed.) San Francisco: Jossey-Bass, 2006.

Carver, J., and Oliver, C. *Corporate Boards That Create Value: Governing Company Performance from the Boardroom.* San Francisco: Jossey-Bass, 2002.

Carver, M., and Charney, B. *The Board Member's Playbook: Using Policy Governance to Solve Problems, Make Decisions, and Build a Stronger Board.* San Francisco: Jossey-Bass, 2004.

Clemmer, J. "Change Management Can Lead to Rigidity and Resistance to Change." Kitchener, Ontario: Clemmer Group, n.d. http://www.clemmer.net/articles/Change_management_Taking_advantage_of_the_unforeseeable_opportunities.aspx.

Drucker, P. F. *Management Challenges for the 21st Century.* New York: HarperCollins, 1999.

Eisenhardt, K. M. "Agency Theory: An Assessment and Review." *Academy of Management Review*, 1989, *14*, 369–381.

Einstein, A. *Out of My Later Years.* New York: Philosophical Library, 1950.

Fifth International Conference on Engaging Communities. *Proceedings.* Brisbane, Australia. 2005. http://engagingcommunities2005.org/home.html.

Hillson, D. "Why Risks Turn into Surprises." *Risk Doctor Briefing.* Aug. 2005. http://www.risk-doctor.com/pdf-briefings/risk-doctor16e.pdf.

Horth, D. M., and Palus, C. J. *The Leader's Edge: Six Creative Competencies for Navigating Complex Challenges.* San Francisco: Jossey-Bass, 2002.

Hough, A., McGregor-Lowndes, M., and Ryan, C. "Policy Governance: 'Yes, But Does It Work?'" *Keeping Good Companies: Journal of Chartered Secretaries Australia*, 2004, *56*, 209–212.

Jensen, M., and Meckling, W. "Theory of the Firm: Managerial Behavior, Agency Costs, and Ownership Structure." *Journal of Financial Economics*, 1976, *3*, 305–360.

Kelly, H. M. "Carver Policy Governance in Canada." *Miller Thomson LLP Charities and Not-For-Profit Newsletter.* July 2003. http://www.millerthomson.com/docs/charities_july_2003.pdf.

Medawar, P. B., and Medawar, J. S. *The Life Science.* New York: HarperCollins, 1977.

Mikkelson, B. "Of Cabbages and Kingmakers." 2007. http://www.snopes.com/language/document/govmemo.htm.

Mintzberg, H., Ahlstrand, B., and Lampel, J. *Strategy Bites Back.* London: Financial Times and Prentice Hall, 2005.

Monks, R., and Minow, N. *Corporate Governance.* (2nd ed.) Malden, Mass.: Blackwell, 2001.

Moore, J. *Meaningful Monitoring.* Vol. 1: *REALBoard Tool Kit™.* Calgary, Canada: Governance Coach, 2005.

Oliver, C., and others. *The Policy Governance Fieldbook: Practical Lessons, Tips, and Tools from the Experiences of Real-World Boards.* San Francisco: Jossey-Bass, 1999.

Oliver, C. "The Black Holes in Research on Governance and Governance Models." *Nonprofit Boards and Governance Review,* Mar. 30, 2006. http://charitychannel.com/.

O'Neill, O. "Onora O'Neill on Trust." Introduction to BBC Radio 4, Reith Lecture, 2002. http://www.open2.net/reith2002/onora_oneill_trust_p.html.

Putnam, R. D., and Feldstein, L. M., with Cohen, D. *Better Together: Restoring the American Community.* New York: Simon & Schuster, 2003.

Sanford, L., with Taylor, D. *Let Go to Grow: Escaping the Commodity Trap.* Upper Saddle River, N.J.: Pearson Education, 2005.

Schwarcz, S. L. "Enron and the Use and Abuse of Special Purpose Entities in Corporate Structures." Duke Law School Public Law and Legal Theory Research Paper Series, no. 28. Durham, N.C.: Duke University School of Law, 2002.

Schwarcz, S. L. "Enron and the Use and Abuse of Special Purpose Entities in Corporate Structures." *University of Cincinnati Law Review,* 2002, *70,* 1309–1318.

Scottish Government. *Community Engagement How To Guide.* Communities Scotland. N.d. http://www.ce.communitiesscotland.gov.uk/stellent/groups/public/documents/webpages/scrcs_006693.hcsp.

Spencer, L. J. *Winning Through Participation: Meeting the Challenge of Corporate Change with the Technology of Participation.* Dubuque, Iowa: Kendall/Hunt, 1998.

Surowiecki, J. *The Wisdom of Crowds.* New York: Random House, 2004.

Szent-Gyorgi, A. In I. J. Good (ed.), *The Scientist Speculates.* London: Capricorn Books, 1965.

United Nations. *Globalization and the State*. New York: Department of Economic and Social Affairs, United Nations, 2001. http://unpan1.un.org/intradoc/groups/public/documents/UN/UNPAN012761.pdf.

Willingham, D. T. "Practice Makes Perfect—But Only If You Practice Beyond the Point of Perfection." *American Educator*. Spring 2004. http://www.aft.org/pubs-reports/american_educator/spring2004/cogsci.html.

INDEX

committee vs., 188–189; assessing current roles of, 26; board delegation to, 139–141; governance roles of, 9; means policies defining roles/authority of, 118–120; monitoring Governance Process and Board-Management Delegation, 156–157; Policy Governance transition role of, 168–169; reviewing monitoring reports, 143

Clemmer, J., 71

Cognition: The Thinking Animal (Willingham), 187

Communication; between CEOs and boards, 61–62, 186–187; Policy Governance impact on, 25; tools for owner relations building and, 58–61

Compliance standard; dealing with compliance/noncompliance to, 144–145; establishing, 144

Consensus agreement, 176

Constituent's advocate approach, 16

Corporate Boards That Create Value (Carver and Oliver), 176

Corporate Governance (Monks and Minow), 137

Customers, 47–48

D

Decision making; board capacity for wise, 54; for Policy Governance adoption, 30–31

Delegating for accountability; authority for, 140–141; capacity for, 141; determining clarity when, 139–140

Demsetz, H., 15

Direct board report, 142–143

Drucker, P., 72

E

Einstein, A., 22, 89

Eisenhardt, K. M., 15

Eliot, G., 22

Embarking on Policy Governance. *See* Policy Governance transition

Ends; assigning responsibility for, 6–7; definition of, 77; delegation of, 9; limiting authority to achieve, 7; Policy Governance architecture position of, 88; questions forming organization's, 6; *See also* Strategic Outcomes

Ends control container, 77

Ends policies; defining your destination, 90–95; examples of, 95; monitoring, 105, 146–153, 162; process of developing, 95–106; providing clear direction through, 91; reviewing, 106; tools for, 106–112

Ends Policy Checklist, 104

Ends policy development; drafting ends policies for, 100–104; gathering expert input from staff and board members, 99; gathering input from other boards, 99; gathering owner input for, 98–99; identifying primary information needs for, 97–98; importance of, 95–96; planning the, 96–97; scanning your environment as research for, 99–100; visioning and brainstorming for, 100

Ends policy drafts; addressing ambitions beyond organization vision, 102–103; board agreement on, 104–105; challenges and tips on, 100–101; checklist for, 104; defining the length of your vision in, 101–102; ensuring ends are feasible in, 102; handling controversy over, 105; including your beliefs and philosophy, 103; keeping ends and means clear in, 103; knowing when to stop, 105

Ends policy monitoring; ECO interpretations must relate to whole policy, 147–148; example of, 149–153; interim benchmarks used for, 149; interpretations refining ends policies through, 146–147; key points for, 162; limitations of, 148

Ends policy tools; Ends policy of closely held private corporation, 110; Ends policy for community college, 109; Ends policy for community welfare agency, 106–107; Ends policy for a parks and recreation society, 107–108; Ends policy for public hospital, 109–110; Ends policy for regional library service, 108; visioning techniques, 110–112

Ends questions; 1: what difference do you want to make? 92; 2: whom do you want to affect? 92–94; 3: what level of cost-efficiency do you want to achieve? 94–95

Enron scandal, 16, 172

Environmental scanning; description of, 99–100; questions for, 100

Ethical issue, 129

Ethical test, 129

Executive Limitations; as container for controlling CEO's means, 78, 125–135; delegation of, 9; monitoring, 153–155, 161, 162–163; as policy category, 8; Policy Governance architecture position of, 88

Executive Limitations monitoring; example of, 153–155; key points for, 162–163; overview of, 153; sample report format, 161

Executive Limitations Report, 143

Expert help, 54

External report, 142

External requirements, 135

F

Felder, R. M., 34

Feldstein, L., 58

Financial reports, 73

Flexible management, 71

Funders, 48

Future owner interests, 52

Future Search, 112

Future Search Network, 112

G

Getting started. *See* Policy Governance transition

Global statement, 147

Governance; comparing Policy Governance to other approaches, 17–19; reviewing current board approach to, 14–16; terminology associated with, 17

Governance goals; questionnaires on board, 35; understanding your, 18–19

Governance Process; as container for controlling board means, 78, 116–120; monitoring, 156–157; as policy category, 8; Policy Governance architecture position of, 88

Governor leadership approach, 16

H

Hillson, D., 132

Horth, D. M., 187

Hough, A., 29

I

Independent report, 142

Internal reports, 142

International Policy Governance Association (IPGA), 23, 25

J

Jensen, M., 15

of, 8–9; board vote to adopt, 182; categories of, 8; definition of, 7, 69–70; Ends, 90–112; ground rules for development of, 178; maintaining your, 86–87; means, 113–136; policy control vs., 183; writing comprehensive yet concise, 7–9

Policy containers; board control through, 75–76; designing policies within, 79–86; Ends, 77; means, 77–79

Policy control; ensuring that you have, 8; having policies vs. having, 183; through policy ranges, 82–83; sequencing policy ranges for, 83–84

Policy design; control through policy ranges, 82–83; haphazard control of, 81; ineffective use of time in, 80; monitoring "any reasonable interpretation," 86; muddled accountability in, 81; pitfalls of traditional, 79–80; within policy containers, 79; powerful, 81–82; sequencing policy ranges, 83–84; stopping at appropriate time, 84–86

Policy Governance; answering questions and concerns about, 22–29; architecture of, 88; assessing rewards and costs of changing to, 19–22; bike analogy of, 3, 25, 27, 113–114; chain of accountability provided by, 5; comparison with other governance approaches, 17–19; frequently asked questions about, 23–29; making the decision to use, 30–31; overview of, 1, 2–3, 41–42; registered service mark and rights to, 26–27; reviewing what your board has learned about, 29–30; theory driving, 3–5; See also Policy Governance transition

Policy Governance components; assigning responsibility for making difference, 6–7; compiling concise written policy,

7–8; defining difference your owners want to make, 5–6; delegating within "any reasonable interpretation," 8–9; ensuring difference your owners want, 9; limiting authority, 7

The Policy Governance Fieldbook (Oliver and others), 10

Policy Governance Filter, 204

Policy Governance planning/implementation; agreeing on board policies, 176–178; annual board, 199–201; continual practicing to perfect, 187; defining agreement (consensus), 176; handling concerns brought to the board, 183–186; handling everyday board-CEO communications, 186–187; making any necessary compromises, 182–183; securing your future through, 178–182; transition time frame, 175–176; voting to adopt your policies, 182

Policy Governance system; adaptation of, 27; available research on, 28–29; benefits of using, 9–12; components of, 5–9; flexibility of, 27; functions of, 3; as model, 2; risk associated with, 27–28; transition to, 20, 165–204

Policy Governance system benefits; becoming a real leadership team, 10; being clear about who does what, 11; being seen to be great, 12; getting there faster, 11; getting where you want to go, 10–11; having needed control and freedom, 11; overview of, 9–10

Policy Governance tools; cost of staying without Policy Governance, 37–38; decision-making process for, 32–33; discussion of Policy Governance, 39–40; getting concerns on the table,